PROFITS OF DOOM

MILKING THE API
FOR ALl

ROBERT STRICKLIN

outskirtspress

DENVER, COLORADO

Profits of Doom
Milking the Apocalyptic Cash Cow For All It's Worth
All Rights Reserved.
Copyright © 2012 Robert Stricklin
v2.0

Outskirts Press, Inc.
http://www.outskirtspress.com

ISBN: 978-1-4327-8931-2

Library of Congress Control Number: 2012903875

Outskirts Press and the "OP" logo are trademarks belonging to Outskirts Press, Inc.

PRINTED IN THE UNITED STATES OF AMERICA

For McKenzie, Alex, Addison and Chloe, the hope of a brighter future

Contents

Introduction

"If the world comes to an end, I want to be in Cincinnati. Everything comes there ten years later." – Mark Twain

THE END IS nigh.

Or so we've been warned again and again for time immemorial.

In fact, the end of the world has been "nigh" so many times over the last several thousand years that it's a wonder we're all still alive.

And yet, here we are – still inhabiting this lush, splendiferous planet … still enjoying the fruits of our labor … still coexisting with our neighbors and adversaries (albeit tenuously at times) … still evolving slowly but surely toward a civil society … yet still heeding the worn-out warnings of assorted doomsayers and still worrying that, sooner or later, they might be right.

Since the dawn of recorded history, mankind has grappled with its collective mortality, reluctantly conceding that nothing lasts forever and accepting the inevitability of our existence on Planet Earth eventually coming to a conclusion.

But "eventually" doesn't have quite the same sense of urgency – or cache – as "nigh." Consequently, a combination of irrational superstition, expediency and good, old-fashioned greed has led to a peculiar universal fascination – if not downright obsession – with what is now ominously designated as the End of Days.

Once the stock and trade of fire-and-brimstone spouting religious zealots, this penchant for predicting the apocalypse has in recent decades taken on a new and exceedingly profitable form, becoming a veritable industry unto itself.

Over the last century alone, billions of dollars have been generated by those exploiting end-times hysteria. Whether it's Bible-thumping preachers extorting cash from fearful followers, self-proclaimed prophets who have parlayed their doomsday scenarios into book deals and lucrative lecture tours, or Hollywood producers who know that global disaster spells box office gold, the perpetual eve of destruction has become one hell of an ongoing payday.

Millions of gullible people worldwide have developed a less than healthy fixation with all things apocalyptic. I should know, I was once one of them – hanging on every word from so-called seers and psychics, searching intently for cryptic messages in Biblical scripture, spending my hard-earned discretionary income on books and movies reveling in the spectacle of mass destruction, convincing myself that the day of reckoning was just around the corner, if not at hand, and getting a perverse thrill out of the prospect.

But even a fanatic can be bamboozled just so many times until he realizes the primary motivation – and sheer calculated lunacy – behind the doomsday craze. Eventually, logic and reason wins out over fear and hysteria, and one sees the positive advantages of choosing to focus on making the world a better place – instead of dwelling on its shortcomings, throwing in the towel and submissively anticipating its demise.

The purpose of this book is two-fold: to expose – in a scathingly light-hearted manner – the dubious and self-serving enterprise that is latter-day prophecy, and to allay any fears you may have that, indeed, the end is imminent based on misinformation or the abysmal track record of false prophets, deluded Biblical scholars and other assorted charlatans and hucksters out to make a less than honest buck.

In the course of this exposé, we'll examine the history of apocalyptic mania from the oracular stylings of ancient Biblical prophets to the millennial madness of medieval minds to the modern day commercialization of end times prophecy and speculation.

We'll scrutinize the modus operandi and wild inaccuracies of a number of colorful – and in some cases shameless – individuals who have achieved fame, if not considerable fortune, with their outlandish predictions of worldwide destruction.

We'll debunk the more popular theories and scenarios advanced by those who keep moving the proverbial doomsday goal posts to perpetuate one of the greatest scams in human history.

And we'll assess the monetary scope of this highly profitable enterprise that has spread like a social disease from tongue to parchment to pulpit to newsprint to celluloid to video to cyberspace – and threatens to reach critical mass in the year 2012.

Sorry to be a party pooper, but with yet another death watch for Planet Earth approaching on December 21, 2012 (the purported end of the Mayan calendar) my mission is to inject a little rational perspective into the public consciousness, put your mind at ease, and turn more than a few naïve Doomsday disciples into level-headed skeptics.

I accept this assignment cognizant of the fact that it could be argued that this book itself is exploiting the apocalypse for fun and profit. Be that as it may, the only defense I can offer is that it's a dirty job … but somebody's got to do it.

CHAPTER **1**

Party Like It's 999

"Don't they know it's the end of the world?" – Arthur Kent and Sylvia Dee (recorded by Skeeter Davis)

IT WAS THE turn of the millennium – the threshold of an uncertain new era – and people throughout the civilized world were convinced that the end times were nigh.

Some pointed to mysterious signs in the heavens. Some were fixated on ominous prophecies in ancient scripture. Some relied on the learned counsel of local clergy or fell under the spell of self-appointed soothsayers whose dire forecasts of apocalypse and the Last Judgment seemed all too credible in a world filled with conflict and transgression. And others were simply predisposed to believing whatever they were told to believe.

In the midst of this mania, there was a revival of religious fervor. Devout Christians flocked to their parishes to make peace with their God. Many divested of their worldly possessions in the hope of earning a place in heaven. Some made pilgrimages to the Holy Land to get a front row seat for the return of the Messiah on the summit of Mount Zion – and many who ventured there did not come back.

Sounds a little like the world on the cusp of 1999-2000 A.D. but, in fact, the date in question was 999 A.D. *Or so the legend goes.* I add this disclaimer because historians are at odds with each other over whether the alleged hysteria actually occurred or is the stuff of folklore, fermented over the centuries like a heady brew.

The popular version of this saga has it that the Christian world of the 10th century was resigned to the belief that the Last Judgment was imminent. And why wouldn't they think the End of Days was approaching? After all, a portion of the Apocrypha – the 15 books or parts of books of the Bible written between 200 B.C. and 100 A.D. – had prophesied that the world would come to an end 1,000 years after the birth of Christ.

Western Europe was still in the waning days of the Dark Ages – dark as in no education, no skills, no culture, no hope and no future beyond the next day, just the opiate of religion and the shallow promise of a better existence in the next life. Who wouldn't want the world to end and cling to the hope of eternal paradise in the after-life?

Also, the seeds of the First Crusade (launched in 1096) were being sowed in Asia Minor with the control of Palestine by Muslims setting the stage for a medieval Armageddon.

And, on top of everything, 999 inverted was the dreaded 666, the number of the beast, the mark of the Antichrist prophesized in the Book of Revelation.

In the fertile imagination of the medieval mind, it was as if The Four Horseman of the Apocalypse – pestilence, war, famine and death – had been unleashed upon the world. Never mind that all four of these woes have always been a part of the human experience. To these fanatics, all the proverbial ducks were in a row.

Reportedly, the Catholic Church under the reign of Pope Sylvester II sought to discourage public expectations of the Day of Reckoning, but to little avail. Apparently, there's something about new millennia that brings out the fear and paranoia in the less than enlightened masses. Which is ironic, considering that the end of one thousand year period and the beginning of another ought to have represented a fresh start, an opportunity to abandon old superstitions ... and replace them with new ones.

But that's not how the simple folk of 999 greeted the milestone.

Instead of celebrating a new era, they poured into churches to pray and beg for absolution. Those with any worldly possessions to their name donated them to the poor. Some were not as generous and, instead, hoarded grain or high-tailed it to higher ground. And many of those who made tracks for Jerusalem died of starvation along the way, inadvertently fulfilling their own end of the world prophecy.

At least, that's one side of the story.

The contrarian view to this recounting maintains that tales of mass suicides, self-flagellation and panic over the least little natural occurrence (comets, earthquakes, floods, hail storms and the like) have been wildly exaggerated over the centuries – or at least embellished with age.

One of the most vehement contradictions was documented by Hillel Schwartz in his 1990 book, *Century's End: A Cultural History of the fin de siècle from the 990's through the 1990's*, in which he wrote:

> *None of this is true. Not the suicides, not the flaming swords, not the whips. Not the absolution, or the parole, nor the forgiveness of debts. Not the mass hysteria, the fatalism, the nightmare, the terror of the number itself. Not the families abandoned …by an army of pilgrims, nor the wealth divested … And no mechanical clocks to strike the midnight hour at millennium's end, no hallelujah choruses at a minute past twelve. None of it – at least according the last hundred years of scholarship.*

That may have indeed been the case, but knowing human nature – and medieval superstition being what it was – surely there was *some* consternation and irrational behavior prevalent, if not of epic proportions.

What we do know for sure is that the world did not end in 999 or in 1000 A.D. or the thousand years that followed. But that hasn't stopped countless similar examples of irrational hysteria from occurring with consistent regularity.

For example, in 1184 A.D., a document known as the Toledo

Letter appeared in England and purported to provide a timetable for the second coming of Christ. According to the letter, a portentous conjunction of the planets indicated that the world would end in September 1186. Exactly who wrote the letter was never made clear, but it ultimately reached the Archbishop of Canterbury who was sufficiently convinced of its veracity that he ordered his followers to observe a three-day fast as a sign of penitence to the great Almighty.

Needless to say, September 1186 proved uneventful as well. But it did not dissuade those who still believed in the letter's warning. Consequently, the letter remained in circulation for several more centuries with the date of doomsday – and other minor details – adjusted accordingly.

Something similar occurred in the early fifteenth century. The Taborites of Bohemia – a religious sect labeled heretical by the Catholic Church – held to the belief that following the defeat of their persecutors, Christ would return in February 1420 and establish his kingdom on Earth from Mount Tabor, a peak south of Prague. They also predicted that every city in the world would be destroyed by fire and only several mountain fortresses would be spared. When the King of Kings failed to show on the appointed date, the Taborites offered a convenient explanation – Christ actually *had* returned, but just decided to remain hidden. And in response to those who doubted their fervent claims, the testy Taborites waged civil war against the German Army for the next 32 years until they were finally vanquished.

If nothing else, these early accounts of doomsday hysteria indicate a persistent fascination with – and a proclivity toward – global annihilation. Call it a collective death wish. It would only be a matter of time until the exploitation of this fear and fascination would become an ongoing enterprise.

Mind you, in 999, there was no such thing as a printing press – just a handful of monks ensconced in a remote monastery with plume pens and a dollop of ink. No telegraph, no radio, no TV or Internet – the tools by which future agent provocateurs would spread the myths and perpetuate the madness of apocalyptic fervor. Had the media existed in the 10th century, one can only imagine the feeding frenzy that would have ensued in bold-type headlines, streaming breaking news, hyperventilating commentary and titillating teasers.

Instead, it was strictly a word-of-mouth phenomenon, the off-shoot of centuries of religious indoctrination. And until technology – and avarice – caught up with the obsession, religious belief based on archaic scripture would have to serve as the driving force.

CHAPTER 2

'Cause the Bible Tells Me So

"The things that you're liable to read in the Bible – it ain't neces-sarily so." – George Gershwin, Porgy and Bess

ACCORDING TO THE Book of Job, "the Lord gave and the Lord hath taken away." And in the mind of true believers, that goes for the creation of the universe and the inevitable end of times. In fact, nowhere are the seeds of fear and fatalism so deeply rooted than in the Holy Bible.

They don't call it the Good Book for nothing. As if the frightening apocalyptic warnings and visions of the New Testament weren't enough, the Old Testament is chock full of scintillating tales of man's sinful ways and the Almighty's terrifying retribution.

Take, for example, the story of Noah. As every child reared in the Judeo-Christian or Islamic cultures knows, Noah was a righteous man who had the misfortune of living in a corrupt society. God took a shine to him, but was extremely displeased with his contemporaries. So he instructed Noah to build an ark and gather not only his own kin but also two of every kind of animal and safely sail out the mother of all storms. It rained for 40 days and 40 nights and the ensuing flood waters engulfed and destroyed everyone on the planet except Noah, his family and his floating menagerie. When the waters eventually receded and the ark came to rest on the side of a mountain, the world began anew. And God vowed that he would never wipe out humanity again with a flood – but didn't rule out a nuclear holocaust, killer asteroids or a supernova.

True to his word, the Almighty chose a different weapon of mass destruction a bit later in dealing with a pair of hotbeds of lasciviousness – Sodom and Gomorrah. Seems those two towns were more perverse than pre-World War II Berlin and pre-Rudy Giuliani Manhattan combined. Disgusted, God brought down fire and brimstone from the sky, but not before his angels alerted Lot – another relatively righteous dude – and allowed him to evacuate his family. There was one caveat – no one was allowed to look back at the spectacle. Unable to resist sneaking a peek, Lot's wife did look back – and turned into a pillar of salt. Bummer.

In the book of Exodus, God unleashed 10 plagues on Egypt when Pharaoh refused to let Moses and the Hebrew slaves go. These curses included:

- Water turned to blood, thus killing all the fish in the Nile river;
- Frogs;
- Lice;
- Disease on livestock (West Nile? Mad cow?);
- Boils;
- Hail mixed with fire;
- Locusts;
- Darkness; and
- Death of all first-borns – unless your doorpost was marked with lamb's blood.

While this didn't necessarily constitute an apocalypse for the land of Egypt, the retelling of this tribulation – especially each year at Passover – has helped to put the fear of God in millions and has led to speculation on what other forms of torture the Almighty might have in store for transgressors in the future.

The first Biblical "clues" as to the possible fate of mankind come in The Book of Daniel – specifically in a series of oracular visions. Daniel was a Judean exile who became a revered government official in the court of Nebuchadnezzar II, who ruled Babylon more than 500 years before the birth of Christ. Daniel proved to be a wise, resourceful and valuable asset to the King – especially when it came to interpreting dreams.

In Chapter 7, Daniel reveals the first of several visions – that of four great beasts representing four future kingdoms, the last of which would conquer the entire earth. The fourth beast has 10 horns which represent 10 kings. Along comes a "little horn" or wicked king who subdues three of the 10 kings, speaks against God and wages war against his saints, and attempts to modify existing law. The wicked king is eventually vanquished and "one like a son of man" assumes worldwide dominion.

Daniel's second vision, described in Chapter 8, initially concerns Persia and Greece, represented by a ram and a goat, respectively. The goat assumes great power until its horn breaks off and is replaced by four "lesser" horns. Also, a wicked king arises and challenges the will of God by removing the daily temple sacrifice and desecrating the temple for "twenty three hundred evenings and mornings."

The third vision is known as the 70-week prophecy and addresses the destruction of Jerusalem and the Holy Temple. This is one of the most contentious prophecies in the Bible because of disagreement over whether Daniel is actually talking about 70 weeks, 70 years or 490 years when he speaks of a period of "seventy sevens." Whatever the time frame, modern-day alarmists have used it to approximate what they believe to be the Great Tribulation, Armageddon and the Second Coming.

The fourth vision focuses on conflicts involving the "King of the North" and the "King of the South," which modern Biblical scholars liberally interpret as Russia and Egypt – or Arab nations in general, although for all we know it could apply to any nations – well, North and South.

These four visions form the basis for the elaborate Doomsday scenario and timeline concocted by a host of modern-day evangelicals. But more about that later.

The prophecies of Ezekiel and Isaiah provide more fodder for End Times enthusiasts. In Chapter 37, Ezekiel writes: *"In the day that I shall cleanse you from all your iniquities, and shall cause the cities to be inhabited, and shall repair the ruinous places, and the desolate land shall be tilled, which before was waste in the sight of all that passed by, they shall say: This land that* was untilled *is become as a garden of pleasure: and the cities that were abandoned, and desolate, and destroyed, are people and fenced."* (36; 33-35) Interpretation: The state of Israel would be established.

Elsewhere, the prophet writes: *"And it shall come to pass in that day, in the day of Gog upon the land of Israel, saith the Lord God, that my indignation shall come up in my wrath.* (38: 18) *… in that day there shall be a great commotion upon the land of Israel … every man's sword shall be pointed against his brother. And I will judge him with pestilence, and with blood, and with violent rain, and vast hailstones: I will rain fire and brimstone upon him, and upon his army, and upon the many nations that are with him."* (38: 19-22) Popular interpretation: There will be hell to pay when Gog (Russia?) and its allies seek to invade Israel.

Similarly – but at much greater length – the Book of Isaiah spends 39 chapters prophesying doom for a sinful Judah, as well as great tribulation for other nations that oppose God, while the last 27 chapters envision the restoration of an Israeli nation and the future establishment of God's kingdom on Earth.

Possible future events have also been cherry-picked from portions of Isaiah and other Old Testament prophets, including:

- As a prelude to the End Times, the Israeli nation would be reestablished (Horsea 3: 4-5).
- During the End Times the Kingdom of God will be established in Jerusalem (Isaiah 2: 2-3).
- *"All nations that have fought against Jerusalem …"* will be consumed by *"the plague …"* (Zacharias 14: 12-13)

Things get even more prophetic – or more cryptic, depending on your point of view – in The New Testament.

In Acts, the Apostle Peter declares that God would pour out his spirit on all people and show signs in the heavens and on the earth before the Second Coming of Christ (Acts 2: 17-20).

In the Gospels according to St. Matthew and Mark, signs of the last day come directly from Jesus who warns: *"And as it was in the days of Noah, even so will be the coming of the Son of Man. For as in the days before the flood they were eating and drinking, marrying and giving in marriage until the day when Noe entered the ark ..."* (Matthew 24: 38) and *"But in those days, after that tribulation, the sun will be darkened, and the moon will not give her light, and the stars of heaven will be falling, and the powers that are in heaven will be shaken."* (Mark 13: 24-25)

And, of course, there is The Book of Revelation – St. John the Apostle's fever dream of visions that have been copiously applied to the End Times – a veritable cornucopia of mysterious symbols and assorted calamities, rambling admonishments and gibberish that has been construed as a grand blueprint for the fate of humanity. Highlights include a series of tribulations – similar to the 10 plagues of Egypt, but on a greater scale – followed by the rise of a false prophet and a beast (an implied Antichrist), Armageddon and the New Jerusalem (heaven on earth).

As if these ancient prophecies aren't enough, creative minds with a lot of time on their hands have invented The Bible Code (aka The Torah Code), a series of prophetic messages alleged to be implanted within the scriptures. These encrypted messages are decoded using the Equidistant Letter Sequence (ELS) method in which the decipherer chooses a starting point and a skip number, and then select letters from the text at equal spacing as given by the skip number – kind of like the word search in your weekend newspaper.

The origin of this preoccupation dates back to the 13th century and a Spanish rabbi named Bachya Ben Asher, but few examples of actually prophetic messages were discovered until the mid-20th century.

In 1994, the mathematical team of (Doron) Witctum, (Eliyahu) Rips and (Yoar) Rosenberg published a paper entitled *Equidistant Letter Sequence in the Book of Genesis* and opened a fresh can of worms.

While a variety of mathematicians and Jewish scholars argued over the validity of the paper and the experiments on which it was based, journalist Michael Drosnin swooped in and published *The Bible Code* in 1997. Filled with numerous examples of past events (World War I, World War II, the Gulf War, JFK assassination) allegedly foretold in the Torah, the book was a runaway bestseller. Naturally, it was followed by a sequel, the equally controversial and lucrative *Bible Code II: The Countdown* in 2002. What undoubtedly spurred sales of the book was its encoded future predictions, which included an attack on the United States by terrorists using nuclear weapons supplied by Libya (which ended its nuclear program in 2003); the assassination of Palestinian leader Yasser Arafat (he died of natural causes in 2004); and an atomic holocaust in 2006. Not only have these wrong predictions created doubts about the Bible Code itself, but Drosnin's subsequent theory that the Code might have been conceived by aliens has only undermined its credibility.

There are, of course, many editions of the Bible – from the King James Version to the New World Translation – and many ways in which its verses are presented and interpreted. For example, the Book of Revelation is known in the Catholic religion as The Apocalypse. But if most of the world's organized religions have one common belief, it is that the world will end perhaps with a bang, but definitely not a whimper.

Here's how each of the major denominations believe the End Times will play out:

Christians, Jews and Muslims are all on the same page when it comes to believing in the return/arrival of a Messiah, Mashiach or Imam Mahdi. Christians and Muslims both await the return of Jesus and a final judgment.

The Quran and Sunnah weigh in on the End Times, pointing to a number of startling signs including the coming of an Antichrist, the

Sun rising in the West instead of the East, an earthquake so powerful that it will crumble mountains, volcanoes that will be caused by the stretching of the earth's crust, the destruction of crops and animals, and the oceans drying up.

Each of these religions provides a compelling reason for believers to tow the line and keep coming back for more: To reject the authority of the religion – and fail to provide for its support – is to risk eternal damnation.

Various other sects have elaborate, differing scenarios regarding the End Times. In Judaism, for example, The End of Days is referred to several times in the Tanakh. Rather than being depicted as the end of humanity, it is seen as the overturn of the established world order marked by turbulent events:

> *"And it shall come to pass in the last days, that the mountain of the LORD's House shall be established in the top of the mountains, and shall be exalted above the hills; and all nations shall flow unto it. And many people shall go and say, Come ye, and let us go up to the mountain of the LORD, to the house of the God of Jacob; and he will teach us of his ways, and we will walk in his paths: for out of Zion shall go forth the law, and the word of the LORD from Jerusalem. And he shall judge among the nations, and shall rebuke many people; and they shall bat their swords into plowshares, and their spears into pruning hooks: nation shall not lift up sword against nation, neither shall they learn war anymore."*
> (Isaiah 2:1-5, King James Version)

As for the timing of this Messianic Era, the Messiah must arrive before the year 6000 from the time of creation – according to the Talmud, the Midrash and the Zohar (Kabala). The year 2011 corresponds to the year 5771 from creation – so we're looking at anywhere from 2011-2240.

Christians, on the other hand, see nothing but trouble just prior to the Messianic Era:

"For then shall be great tribulation, such as was not since the be-ginning of the world to this time, no, nor ever shall be. And except those days should be shortened, there should no flesh be saved: but for the elect's sake those days shall be shortened." (Matthew 14:15-22, King James Version).

Luke 21:20-33 – "And when ye shall see Jerusalem compassed with armies, then know that the desolation thereof is nigh … Jerusalem shall be trodden down of the Gentiles … And there shall be signs in the sun, and in the moon, and in the stars; and upon the earth distress of nations with perplexity; the sea and the waves roaring; Men's hearts failing them for fear, and for looking after those things which are coming on the earth; for the powers of heaven shall be shaken. And then shall they see the Son of man coming in a cloud with power and great glory."

Despite their portrayal in movies like *The Omen*, the Catholic clergy generally adheres to a non-literal fulfillment of Biblical proph-ecy as espoused by Augustine of Hippo in his 5th century book, *The City of God.* They do acknowledge the warning signs of the End Times foretold by Jesus when he spoke of "wars and rumors of wars," among other calamities. However, they avoid setting even an approximate date for the Apocalypse, preferring the vague forewarning that it will arrive like a "thief in the night." (I Thessalonians 5:2)

Protestant Christians are not as timid when it comes to speculat-ing on the time, place and circumstances of the End Times. The only debate is whether the Rapture occurs before or after the Tribulation. In this regard, there are even several different schools of thought:

- Fundamentalists believe that Biblical prophecy will be fulfilled literally. In fact, they are convinced that current world events – including regional wars, natural disasters and famines – rep-resent the "birth pains" alluded to by Jesus in Matthew 24: 7-8 and Mark 13:8. They also believe Meggido is where the world as we know it will come to an end and that Jesus will establish a kingdom on Earth for 1,000 years.

- Millenialists believe that there will be a 1000-year Golden Age of heaven on earth established by the second coming of Christ prior to the Last Judgment.
- Amillenialists maintain that the end times encompasses the period from Christ's ascension to the Last Judgment and will not be literally fulfilled, especially the reference to Christ's thousand-year reign on Earth in the Book of Revelation.
- Premillenialists believe that Jesus Christ will return prior to his literal reign on Earth for 100 years. They contend that the End Times are happening here and now, offering specific timelines leading to the end of the world. In the world view of many of these true believers, Israel, the European Union or the United Nations are key players whose roles – they believe – have been foretold in Biblical scriptures. Premillenialists are made up of three groups:
  - » Pre-tribulationists believe the Rapture will occur prior to the seven-year tribulation, but not necessarily immediately before the Tribulation.
  - » Mid-tribulationists believe the Rapture will occur three and a half years into the tribulation at the beginning of the three-and-a-year great tribulation.
  - » Post-tribulationists believe the Rapture will not occur until the end of the seven-year tribulation just prior to the beginning of the millennial kingdom.
- Dispensational premillenialists believe that Christians will be suddenly whisked away to Heaven (the Rapture) prior to the Great Tribulation.

Things get a little more complicated for the Seven-day Adventists, who believe that the Bible foretells a situation in which the United States works in unison with the Catholic Church to mandate worship on another day besides the seventh-day Sabbath (Saturday) in violation of the Ten Commandments.

Mormons, members of the Church of Jesus Christ of Latter-day Saints, are taught that mankind is currently living in the last days. Some Mormon leaders believe that we have been allotted seven thousand years on the planet and the earth is approaching the end of its sixth millennium. The seventh thousandth year, they maintain, will witness the Second Coming and will usher in Christ's 1000-year kingdom on Earth. Furthermore, the seven seals and seven seals referred to in the Book of Revelation relate to this seven-millennium period.

According to the Jehovah's Witnesses, the last days commenced in 1914 with the events that triggered World War I. At some future date, God will cleanse the earth of all sin and Satan will be restrained for 1,000 years. During this golden era, the dead will be resurrected and given the opportunity to know God and live again under the rule of Jesus Christ who – along with 144,000 co-rulers – will restore the Earth to its original, long-lost paradise state. In such a world, there will be peace, harmony and no more death or illness.

The good news for Hindus is that there are no End Times in their religion. Neither is there a Hell. Rather than believing in an event-specific timeline, Hindus embrace a cyclic perception of external history and an internal spirituality. Their faith is based on the concept of a Kalpa (cycle) spanning 8.64 billion years and illustrating a pattern of decline in the state of nature and civilization between epochs of timelessness when Brahma (the Creator) regenerates existence and reality. This process is comprised of four yugas (ages) that start with complete purity and end with complete impurity. The last is Kali Yuga, an evil, dark age in which nature is decayed and civilization has become spiritually degraded and violence and disease shorten human lives. This results in complete destruction followed by Satya Yuga, a golden era where everyone is righteous – followed by other yugas until another Kali Yuga comes along. In other words, these epochs keep repeating *infinitely*.

Like Hindus, Buddhists generally believe in an endless cycle of creation and destruction. For them, the current epoch in which we live merely represents the latest step. In fact, the founder of Buddhism

– Gautama Buddha – predicted that his teachings would disappear after 5,000 years and that no one would practice Buddhism at that time.

In the final stage before renewal, according to the Sutta Pitaka, the "ten moral courses of conduct" will fade away and people will indulge in the ten amoral concepts of theft, violence, murder, lying, evil speaking, adultery, abusive and idle talk, covetousness and ill will, wanton greed and perverted lust – which sounds like an average day in our modern world. It is believed that the era culminating in the arrival of the next Buddha Maitreya will be epitomized by impiety, physical weakness, sexual depravity and social disorder.

So in one form or another, all of the major religions – and the billions of people who subscribe to them – support the belief of inevitable worldwide upheaval or apocalyptic change. But those who rely on the Christian Bible as their primary source of guidance are clearly the most receptive to the notion of an apocalypse by intelligent design.

In order to be so, one must unequivocally accept that the Bible is the undisputed word of God – and not the biased, uninformed and sometimes irrational ruminations of a single, ancient individual whose verses have been translated and modified repeatedly over the course of several millennia. That's a pretty tall order and a tremendous leap of faith.

So why do so many educated and seemingly enlightened people literally buy into detailed end-times scenarios based on faulty interpretations of archaic scriptures? Because they *want* to believe them. Because it gives their existence meaning, purpose and something to look forward to with a mixture of apprehension, fascination and resolve.

Like numerous myths and legends throughout history that have endured because they've held generations spellbound and sparked the imagination, the End Times offer the ultimate saga, complete with a hero (Jesus/God) and a villain (the Antichrist/Satan), an intriguing back story (Genesis), compelling chapters (the life and death of

Christ, the Rapture and the rise of an Antichrist) an amazing climax (Armageddon and the Second Coming) and an epilogue (the new Jerusalem) – making it the greatest bedtime story ever foretold.

And although the last of the Biblical prophecies was written 2000 years ago, here we are in the 21st century, still awaiting their fulfillment. In the years since St. John penned his Book of Revelation, there have been many would-be prophets who have attempted to follow in his footsteps, but only succeeded in perpetuating fallacies and paving the way for the most lucrative scam in human history.

Let's identify some of these second-hand soothsayers and architects of absurdity …

CHAPTER 3

Seer Suckers

"Among all forms of mistake, prophecy is the most gratuitous." –
George Eliot

IF, AS SOME say, prostitution is the world's oldest profession, then prognostication is surely the second oldest, dating back to Egyptian times in the form of hieroglyphics and later refined in Greek mythology with the Oracle of Delphi and Biblical scripture with the likes of Ezekiel and Isaiah.

In later years, it didn't take long for self-professed psychics and soothsayers to realize they could make a name for themselves and/ or build a following by preying on the public's innate fear of an uncertain future.

Over the centuries, a plethora of would-be prognosticators emerged – some rather colorful, others certifiable, and even a few who may or may not have even existed but whose alleged prophecies served the purpose of whipping the citizenry into a self-righteous frenzy.

Take St. Malachy. Born in Armagh, Ireland in 1094, Mael Maedic Ua Morgair grew up to become Archbishop of Armagh. Credited with several miracles, he was canonized by Pope Clement III as the first Irish saint. But his real claim to fame is his alleged prophecies regarding the papacy. In 1139, while visiting Pope Innocent II in Rome,

Malachy purportedly envisioned the identities of all future popes and antipopes – 112 to be exact – and described each of them in short phrases or mottoes.

For example, Alexander III (1159-1181) was assigned the motto, "Ex anfere cuftode," Latin for "Out of the guardian goose." Oddly enough, the family coat of arms of Alexander III, aka Orlando Bandinelli Paparoni, had a goose on it. His immediate successor, Lucius III, was referred to as "Lux in oftio" or "A light in the entrance." Lux is an obvious play on the word Lucius. And so forth down the line to modern times.

Pope John Paul II, the 110th pope on Malachy's list, was identified as "De labore solis" or "Of the labor of the sun." Several explanations have been given for this assignation. One of the more plausible is that Karol Jozef Woityla was born on the same day as a partial solar eclipse over the Indian Ocean and buried on the day of a rare hybrid eclipse over the South Pacific and South America.

According to St. Malachy, the 111th pontiff would be known as "Gloria olivae" or "glory of the olive." The olive is the symbol of the Order of Saint Benedict. Was it fate or design that led Joseph Cardinal Ratzinger, not a Benedictine, to adopt the name Pope Benedict XVI? And what are we to make of St. Malachy's additional prophecy about this pontiff? *"He will reign during the ultimate persecution of the Holy Roman Church."*

Does this refer to allegations that Pope Benedict XVI knew of efforts to cover up the Church's pedophilia scandal?

Since St. Malachy's vision included 112 future pontiffs, the belief is that the next pope will be the last. His name, according to Malachy, will be "Petrus Romanus" or "Peter the Roman," like St. Peter, the first pope – an appropriate designation because it would bring the papacy full circle. His is the longest motto – actually an ominous prophecy – that, in English, roughly translate as:

"In the last persecution of the Holy Roman Church, Peter the Roman will hold the see, who will pasture his sheep in many

tribulations: and when these things are finished, the city of seven hills (Rome) will be destroyed, and the terrible judge will judge his people. The End."

Standard interpretation – once Benedict XVI kicks the bucket, the last pope will oversee a world of trouble, followed by the destruction of Rome (and presumably many other cities around the globe) and the Last Judgment.

Yikes! Sure sounds like the Apocalypse – and in the not-too-distant future. As one would expect, a number of Doomsday profiteers have made the case – based on the seeming accuracy of St. Malachy's previous prophecies – that the proverbial writing is on the wall. But there is one hitch with these prophecies – many scholars are not convinced that St. Malachy actually wrote them.

For one thing, after Saint Malachy allegedly presented his manuscript to Innocent II the document was placed in the Roman Archives where it went undiscovered until 1590. During that 450-year period, no one had any knowledge that the prophecies existed – not even St. Bernard de Clairvaux, the author of the "Life of St. Malachy" in the 12th century. That alone casts some doubt as to their authenticity. In his *Teatro Critico Universal* (1724-1739), Spanish author Father Benito Jerónimo Feijóo claimed the prophecies were indeed a forgery designed to influence the selection of the next pontiff after Urban VII since the first time the prophecies came to light was on a handwritten account by patriarch Alfonso Chacon – who unsuccessfully championed the candidacy of one Cardinal Girolamo Simoncelli in 1590.

Even if the prophecies were authentic, their "uncanny" accuracy is questionable. The mottoes allude to a wide range of traits, insignias, countries of origin, titles and symbols that are open to interpretation and could apply to virtually any Pope in some way, shape or form. In other words, if the motto doesn't necessarily fit the Pope, some connection can be found to make the Pope fit the motto.

St. Malachy was but the first in a long line of religious figures with apocalyptic notions. Consider the case of Brother Arnold – an ex-Dominican monk who, in 1260, didn't exactly ingratiate himself with the Vatican by stating his belief that the current Pope was the Antichrist, the church was essentially corrupt, and it was all a sign of the times – the End Times. He did, however, manage to build a large following of believers who were rather disappointed when his predictions of Doomsday failed to materialize and, consequently, abandoned him.

Then there was Mother Shipton, aka Ursula Sonthiel Shipton, who according to legend was born in Yorkshire, England in 1488 as the sire of a country maiden and Satan himself. Legend also has it that she was hideously ugly and eventually aspired to a profession befitting a hideously ugly woman – she became a fortuneteller. Eighty years after her death in 1561, a compilation of her alleged prophecies were printed. Mother Shipton had a way with rhyme that rivals today's best hip-hop rappers. Check out this ditty:

"A carriage without horse will go, disaster fill the world with woe." (As in, a horseless carriage? The automobile?)

Or this one: *"Around the world men's thoughts will fly, faster than the twinkle of an eye."* (The telegraph? E-mail?)

It gets better. Here's more:

"Beneath the water, men shall walk, shall ride, shall sleep, shall even talk."

"In water, iron then shall float, as easy as a wooden boat."

"Gold shall be seen in stream and stone, in land that is yet unknown."

"For in those wondrous far off days, the women shall adopt a craze, to dress like men, and trousers wear, and to cut off their locks of hair."

"And roaring monsters with men atop, does seem to eat the verdant crop. And men shall fly as birds do now, and give away the horse and plow."

Of course, these are just some of the more cheerful prophecies attributed to Mother Shipton. Naturally, there is one long rambling "rap" that paints a bleaker picture of the fate of the world. Here are a few excerpts:

"When pictures seem alive with movements free,
When boats like fishes swim beneath the sea,
When men like birds shall scour the sky,
Then half the world, deep drenched in blood shall die."

"A fiery dragon will cross the sky
Six times before the earth shall die.
Mankind will tremble and frightened be
For the six heralds in this prophecy."

"Not every soul on earth will die,
As the dragon's tail goes sweeping by,
Not every land on earth will sink,
But these will wallow in stench and stink,
Of rotting bodies of beast and man,
Of vegetation crisped on land."

"The dragon's tail is but a sign
For mankind's fall and man's decline …"

Well, now we know who was Dr. Seuss' poetic muse.

Unfortunately, many now believe that Mother Shipton and her gift of prophecy were merely the stuff of legend. For one thing, the first published book of her verses did not appear until 1641 – 80 years after her death. Her "biography" was published in 1684, but it is believed that author Richard Head invented or embellished the details of her life. Another edition of Mother Shipton's work was published in 1862 with her most elaborate prediction supposedly forged by Charles Hindley. And even if Mother Shipton had written the predictions attributed to her, how could she live down this one:

"The world to an end shall come
In eighteen hundred and eighty one."

Good night, Mother.

On the other hand, there is no question that Johannes Stoeffler existed. A German astrologer, Stoeffler was held in high regard as an exceedingly learned man who taught at the Tubigen University. That is until he made this prediction: "The world will end by a giant flood on February 20, 1524." Coincidentally, one of Europe's worst storms arrived on that fateful day and hundreds of people died desperately fleeing to the local harbor and their feeble watercrafts. But the storm eventually blew over, the world remained, and – like many modern day weathermen – Stoeffler's reputation as a prognosticator was all washed up.

Then in 1527, a German bookbinder with the appropriate name of Hans Nut announced that he was the Second Coming of the Messiah. Somehow he developed a rabid cult following and began warning that the end was near. Actually, he was right. For no sooner did his predictions fail than his fanatics folded their tents and he was thrown into prison by the Catholic Church, where he died while trying to escape. Talk about bad karma.

Then there was Ann Lee, or Mother Ann and Ann the Word, as she was called by the United Society of Believers in Christ's Second Appearing, or Shakers for short. In 1774, Ann of a thousand names immigrated to America from her native Manchester, England following a "revelation" and – pardon the pun – really began to shake things up. She claimed to have received a message from God that celibacy and the confession of one's sins were the only true path to eternal salvation and the only way in which the Lord could establish his kingdom on earth.

No doubt Mother Ann's aversion to sexual relations – and matrimony for that matter – stemmed from her forced marriage and eight pregnancies which included four stillbirths and four children who all died before reaching the age of six. Be that as it may, her mission drew a considerable number of converts in the upstate New York and Massachusetts areas. Over time, however, the Shakers have found it hard to sustain a religion that advocates celibacy – particularly in the modern world – and their ranks have dwindled considerably.

When she wasn't talking in tongues, Mother Ann also preached that the Second Coming of Christ was imminent. More than 200 years after her death in 1784, a handful of remaining Shakers are still waiting.

Hopeless anticipation seems to be a common thread among our cavalcade of clumsy clairvoyants. So convinced are they in their prophecies that they cling to them beyond their expiration dates.

That was certainly the case with Herbert Armstrong, founder of the Worldwide Church of God and the Harold Stassen of prophecy, who predicted the end of the world in 1936 … and then again in 1943 and 1972. Obviously a cockeyed pessimist, Armstrong took one last stab at pinpointing the year of reckoning and chose 1986. Armstrong passed away in January, 1986 – the world did not.

It was in the 20th century that prognostication met showbiz and characters like Jeron Criswell Konig were born. Hailing from Princeton, Indiana, Konig attended the University of Cincinnati's Conservatory of Music and toiled in the regional newspaper business before moving to California to become a radio announcer and broadcaster. In the early 1950s, he hosted a series of infomercials for vitamins on a local Los Angeles television station. To help fill time on the program, Konig began offering his predictions of world events – and thus discovered his true calling.

Konig – who became known as Jeron Criswell King, then Jeron King Criswell and then the Amazing Criswell – had more aliases than a snake oil salesman with a personality to match. With his spit-curled, powder white pompadour and a stentorian voice tinged with ominous theatrical foreboding, Criswell sounded like the great and powerful Wizard of Oz (but also had a lot in common with that man behind the curtain). Dressed in a sequined tuxedo to boot, he was the epitome of show business kitsch. To bolster his credentials as a calculated eccentric, he even claimed to sleep in a coffin – a habit he had allegedly acquired back in Indiana working in his family's funeral parlor. Soon enough he became a D-List celebrity in the L.A.-Hollywood milieu, befriending faded movie stars like Mae West and hobnobbing at parties with the likes of George Liberace, Maila Nurmi (Vampira) and the infamous Ed Wood, who cast Criswell in *Plan 9 From Outer Space*, considered by many film critics as the worst movie ever made. As a point of reference, the clique's escapades were amusingly documented in the 1994 Tim Burton film *Ed Wood*.

But it was Criswell's gift of prophecy – or lack thereof – that made him a colorful character. Criswell claimed that his predictions were 87 percent accurate – or as my friend Steve Friedman once quipped, "87 percent accurate 2 percent of the time." Nevertheless, Criswell made a name for himself nationally by appearing frequently on *The Jack Paar Show* and his own program, *Criswell Predicts*.

It was on the Jack Paar TV special in 1963 that Criswell predicted, "President Kennedy will not run for reelection in 1964 because of something that will happen to him in November 1963." He didn't elaborate on what that something would be, but let's not be picky. It was a pretty good guess.

It was followed, however, by quite a few bad guesses, most of them preserved in print in his 1968 book, *Criswell Predicts*. One example: "I predict Fidel Castro will be assassinated on August 9, 1970." The only thing of Castro's that was assassinated was his character when his own daughter later fled Cuba and defected to the United States. Otherwise, the Castro regime remained in power for another 40-plus year. In his old age, Fidel became a Castro Predicts of sorts himself, warning that the United States would trigger World War III by attacking Iran and North Korea. Not even close, and no cigar.

In his tome, Criswell also went on to predict "homosexual cities" in the future, another forecast that has not yet been realized – San Francisco notwithstanding. He also predicted that Ronald Reagan would not seek re-election as California Governor (he did and won), John F. Kennedy Jr. would be elected U.S. Senator from Massachusetts (he might have were it not for his untimely death in 1999), Denver – of all places – would be attacked by a force from outer space, London would be destroyed by a meteor, and cannibalism would ravage Pittsburgh, Pennsylvania in 1980 (inspired perhaps by *Night of the Living Dead,* which was filmed just north of Pittsburgh?).

And let us not forget that he predicted the world would end on August 18, 1999. Although, prior to his death on October 4, 1982, Criswell recanted that prediction and instead asserted the world would end around the winter solstice in 2012, having become an avid aficionado of Mayan culture and taken note of the end of the Mayan calendar. In fact, Criswell may well be the forerunner of the current 2012 Mayan Doomsday cult.

Criswell's shtick may not have made him a millionaire, but it certainly got him plenty of gigs on TV talk shows and a certain level of enduring notoriety. He did appear in four films (*Plan 9, Night of the Ghouls, Orgy of the Dead* and *It Came From Hollywood*) and two documentaries about Ed Wood, penned two books, and had his own syndicated television program. Not bad for a pseudo-psychic who couldn't predict the next day's weather if he tried.

A contemporary of Criswell's – with a much better track record for prognostication – was England's Maurice Woodruff who, in the 1960's, became relatively famous as the "astrologer to the stars." Among many others, his clientele included composer Lionel Bart, actress Diana Dors and, most famously, legendary comic actor Peter Sellers who scarcely made an important personal or professional decision without consulting Woodruff.

Apparently, divination – as well as showmanship – ran in the Woodruff family. Maurice's mother, Vera "Woody" Woodruff was a clairvoyant who paved the way for her son's career as a multimedia soothsayer. As a syndicated newspaper columnist, Woodruff reached 50 million readers and received some 5,000 letters per week. What piqued the interest of so many celebrities and the public alike was the perceived accuracy of Woodruff's predictions, which included the sudden death of John F. Kennedy. He also appeared on stage and in cabarets, authored four books (including his mother's biography), and briefly had his own syndicated American television show in 1969.

In fact, it was on his TV show that Woodruff predicted that America's involvement in the Vietnam War would continue for another several years. He also predicted just prior to Chappaquiddick that Senator Edward Kennedy – a hot political contender at the time – would not be elected President in 1972 or 1976, and probably never at all.

To Mr. Woodruff's credit, he never predicted the end of the world, but deserves to be mentioned as one of the most publicized and gainfully employed psychics of his era. If there was one important event he failed to foresee, however, it was his own death of a massive heart attack in 1973 at the age of 56 while on a lecture tour in Singapore.

In 1996, California psychic Sheldon Nidle went way out on a limb to predict the world would come to end when 16 million space ships (give or take a few) would descend upon the Earth on December 17th – accompanied by an army of angels. Mr. Nidle, perhaps inspired by the release of the alien invasion film *Independence Day* earlier that year, explained that the eventual no-show was because the angels had decided to give mankind a second chance. Awwww ...

But the wackiness of Nidle's predictions paled in comparison to those of Russian scientist Vladimir Sobolyovhas of the Rerikh Academy who, in 1997, released his forecast based on an analysis of prophecies by Nostradamus and a number of Russian saints.

According to Sobolyovhas, the earth's axis would suddenly tilt by approximately 30 degrees by 1999. As a result, the Scandinavian nations and Britain would be underwater. But not to worry, his native Siberia would be spared from devastation. As if that weren't momentous enough, aliens would intervene and lead the surviving inhabitants of the world into – THE FOURTH DIMENSION!

While no doubt being measured for a strait jacket and a padded cell, Sobolyovhas claimed that aliens were already living among us, but were in hiding. "If we completely believed in them," he reasoned, "we would get lazy. So they are clever. They stay hidden in the fourth dimension and only show themselves from time to time."

These are just a handful of the many deluded, self-professed prophets of the post-Biblical age who were either blinded by religious zealotry, desperate for attention, or out to cash in on the gullibility of the masses. Next, we will focus on three of the most popular psychic superstars of the last 500 years whose predictions regarding the End Times have not only fueled many an overactive imagination, but also have lined the pockets of countless biographers, publishers, producers and promoters.

CHAPTER **4**

The Nostradamus Spin Zone

"I am the eyes of Nostradamus, all your ways are known to me."
– Al Stewart

IF THERE IS one post-Biblical seer who has stood the test of time – and generated millions of dollars in publishing and film revenues for people he never knew – it is Michel de Nostradame, the 16th century French apothecary/astrologer whose Latinized last name – Nostradamus – has become synonymous with historic and apocalyptic prophecy.

Born in 1503 in Saint-Rémy-de-Provence, Michel was one of at least nine children, the son of a grain dealer and notary whose family had converted from Judaism to Catholicism some years earlier. A smart move considering the level of anti-Semitism prevalent at the time. By the age of fifteen, Michel was attending the University of Avignon, but was forced to leave a year later during an outbreak of the plague. He traveled throughout the countryside for the next eight years, practicing as an apothecary and researching herbal remedies until he was admitted to the University of Montpelier in 1529, where it was his intention to earn a doctorate in medicine. However, when his past as an apothecary – a trade banned by the university – came to light, Michel was unceremoniously expelled and forced to return to his undervalued occupation.

In 1531, Michel was invited to Agen, a commune in the Aquitaine region of southwestern France by Renaissance scholar Jules-César Scaliger. While there, Michel met and married a woman named Henriette with whom he had two children. But their happiness was short-lived as the plague claimed the lives of Michel's young family in 1534. He took to the road again, traveling through France and Italy until finally settling in Marseille in 1545 to assist physician Louis Serre during yet another outbreak of the plague.

Two years later, Michel remarried – this time to a rich widow named Anne Ponsarde – and began to drift away from the medical profession – and more toward the occult. In 1550, he began publishing annual almanacs under a new name – Nostradamus. Each of these was more popular than the one before it largely because they contained intriguing prophecies.

Soon enough, nobility and others in the upper echelon of society began asking Nostradamus to provide them with personal horoscopes and psychic counseling. The most prominent of these was Catherine de Médici, queen consort of King Henri II of French. The queen was so enamored of Nostradamus that she named him Counselor and Physician-In-Ordinary to her son, who became King Charles IX.

In 1555, Nostradamus published the first installment of his legendary *Les Proheties (The Prophecies),*a collection of oracles dealing with world events from his own time presumably until the end of the world. The second installment appeared in 1557, followed by a third installment in 1558. A complete version of *The Prophecies* was not compiled until after Nostradamus' death in 1566. The volume was divided into 10 chapters (or "centuries") containing 100 hundred quatrains each (except for the unfinished Century VII, which contains only 42 quatrains).

The quatrains are not presented in chronological order, their sequence deliberately disorganized by Nostradamus to puzzle non-initiates (like you and me). The verses are written in French, Italian, Greek and Latin and have been meticulously translated into English by a wide variety of modern historians, notably Charles A. Ward in *Oracles of Nostradamus* (The Modern Library, 1940), Henry C.

Roberts in *The Complete Prophecies of Nostradamus* (originally 1947, Crown Publishers, 1983) and Erika Cheetham in *The Prophecies of Nostradamus* (Capricorn Books, G.P. Putnam's Sons, 1974).

The rap against Nostradamus is that his quatrains are subject to considerable interpretation and, therefore, one can see what one wants to see in them. But let's give credit where credit is due. To envision weapons of mass destruction, global warfare and advanced technology – all of which Nostradamus did – was not an easy task for a man of the 16th century. Nor was it a prudent undertaking considering that era's prevailing intolerance to practices that were perceived as a threat to conventional belief systems. Which is why I am inclined to cut Nostradamus a little slack.

There are two logical reasons why Nostradamus' quatrains are so obscure. One is that many of the seer's visions (or what he believed he envisioned) were beyond the full comprehension of a man living in his time. How would such an Elizabethan fellow process images of an atomic explosion or space flight or airplanes flying into mega-skyscrapers – much less describe them in words?

The other reason is because Nostradamus couldn't afford to name names and provide details of scientific inventions and such without the risk of being branded a heretic. His Jewish roots already made him a potential target for Christian zealots. It's a wonder that the method by which he divined his prophecies – disclosed in his first two quatrains – didn't lead to charges of sorcery:

Sitting alone at night in secret study;
it is placed on the brass tripod.
A slight flame comes out of the emptiness
and makes successful that which should not be believed in vain.

The wand in the hand is placed in the middle of the tripod's legs.
with water he sprinkles both the hem of his garment and his foot.
A voice, fear; he trembles in his robes.
Divine splendor; the god sits nearby.

Of course, these excuses don't necessarily get Nostradamus off the hook. Some quatrains are so vague that they can't be attributed to *any* events. For example, what are we to make of Century VI, Quatrain 41?

The bones of the feet and the hands locked up,
because of the noise the house is uninhabited for a long time.
Digging in dreams they will be unearthed,
the house healthy and inhabited without noise.

Other quatrains – few in number – are amazingly specific, such as the prediction of a great fire in London in 1666:

The blood of the just will be demanded of London
burnt by fire in three times twenty plus six.
The ancient lady will fall from her high position,
and many of the same denomination will be killed.

Most of the quatrains, however, are like little time bombs that won't have significance until events that sort of fit materialize ... eventually. That is the luxury of foretelling events hundreds of years into the future. Sooner or later, they will come to pass. A predicted flood in Lyons will eventually occur. A foretold comet passing during a time of war is a safe bet. Call it Nostradamus' law – whatever could happen, sooner or later will happen. Which is one of the understandable criticisms leveled at Nostradamus by many skeptics.

Nevertheless, because of the apparent accuracy of many of its quatrains and the wide range of events they pertain to, *The Prophecies* have generated more interest than any other source of prophecy including the Biblical forecasts of the Old and New Testaments. Nostradamus' predictions were read with particular interest during World War II when both the Allies and Axis powers used certain quatrains as propaganda. In fact, one of Nostradamus' most accurate predictions (Century II, Quatrain 24) just about names the leader of the Third Reich:

Beasts wild with hunger will cross the rivers,
the greater part of the battlefield will be against Hister,
He will drag the leader in a cage of iron,
When the child of Germany observes no law.

And one can easily read the nuclear bombing of Hiroshima and Nagasaki into Century II, Quatrain 6:

Near the harbor and in two cities
will be two scourges, the like of which have never been seen.
Hunger, plague within, people thrown out the sword
will cry for help from the great immortal God.

Other virtually spot-on predictions included the Kennedy as-sassinations (Century I, Quatrain 26) and the lunar landing of 1969 (Century IX, Quatrain 65):

The great man will be struck down in the day by a thunderbolt.
An evil deed, foretold by the bearer of a petition.
According to the prediction another falls at night time.
Conflict at Reims, London, and pestilence in Tuscany.

He will come to take himself to the corner of Luna,
where he will be taken and placed on foreign land.
The unripe fruit will be the subject of great scandal,
great blame, to the other great praise.

Admittedly, many of Nostradamus' quatrains are obscure and am-biguous. Others fit specific historical events, but are so cryptic and laden with metaphor and symbolism that they depend on the imagi-nation of the reader to discover their relevance. Some of those dealing with developments of the 20th century, however, are so recognizable that it's hard for anyone to completely dismiss Nostradamus' fore-sight. Those concerning the creation of Israel (Century III, Quatrain

97), aerial warfare (Century I, Quatrain 64) and the fall of the Berlin Wall (Century V, Quatrain 81) are good examples.

At this point, let me state that I have no problem with the interest in Nostradamus' prophecies or the prophecies themselves. It is the blatant manipulation and exploitation of Nostradmus' prophecies that get my goat. Much has been lost – or deliberately misconstrued – in translation. The obvious motive is to sensationalize Nostradamus' predictions and force them to become more relevant to our times. Even I have indulged in this gambit.

In the January/February1979 issue of *Gnostica*, I made the case that Nostradamus predicted the mysterious death of Pope John Paul I in Century III, Quatrain 65 which, according to historian Charles A. Ward translates as:

When the tomb of the great Roman shall have been found,
the day after shall be elected a Pontiff
hardly shall he be approved by the Senate
when his blood shall be poisoned in the sacred chalice.

In the same article, I attributed Century VIII, Quatrain 46 to the death of John Paul I's predecessor Pope Paul VI:

Paul the celibate will die three leagues from Rome,
the two nearest flee the oppressed monster,
 When Mars will take up his horrible throne,
the Cock and the Eagle, France and the three brothers.

Here was my rationale:

There were only two Popes named Paul since the days of Nostradamus. We know he is referring to Pail VI (an immovable advocate of celibacy in an age of reform) because he is mentioned in the same breath as "the three brothers" who are universally identified as the Kennedys.

Mars is a reference to war, perhaps the Vietnam War (waged first by France, then the United States, the Cock and the Eagle) or the wave of terrorism that is [at that time] plaguing Italy.

Pope Paul VI reigned from 1963-1978, firmly included in the Kennedy-Vietnam era. The quatrain claims that Paul VI would die a short distance from Rome, but not the Vatican. Paul VI died about thirty miles from Rome. Nostradamus' approximation was amazingly close.

Nostradamus then turns to the surprising choice of Albino Cardinal Luciani over a wide field of likely candidates. In Century III, Quatrain 65, it is revealed:

> *When the tomb of the great Roman shall have been found,*
> *the day after shall be elected a Pontiff:*
> *hardly shall he be approved by the Senate*
> *when his blood shall be poisoned in the sacred chalice.*

The quatrain refers to the discovery of the tomb of a great Roman. During the reign of Pope Paul VI, a tomb was found and suggested as the burial place of St. Peter, the first Pope. Or "The Great Roman" may very likely refer to Pope Paul VI.

> *"...the day after shall be elected a Pontiff ..."*

After Pope Paul VI was entombed, the College of Cardinals set about the task of electing a successor. Although Albino Cardinal Luciani was not elected one day after Pope Paul's funeral, his election came within one day of the start of the conclave.

> *"...hardly shall he be approved by the Senate when his blood shall be poisoned in the sacred chalice ..."*

Hardly had Pope John Paul I been approved by the College of Cardinals, a mere thirty-four days later, when his reign came to an abrupt end. The cause of death was reported as a massive coronary ... This is not to suggest that Pope John Paul I was the victim of foul play inflicted by those who had elected him ... Still, the circumstances of the Pope's death are puzzling. The 65-year-old Pontiff did not have a record of serious health problems and was reportedly in excellent spirits only hours before the fatal attack. He did not complain of chest pains or numbness that often precedes a serious coronary.

Yet, while lying in the comfort of his bed, reading a book, he was suddenly stricken. Despite demands from conservative factions of the Church, the Vatican would not permit a routine autopsy to be performed, a practice that has been carried out on other occasions on other popes. Does the line "his blood shall be poisoned in the sacred chalice"... imply a natural death or assassination? It is all in the interpretation of the reader.

Indeed. Which brings us to two of Nostradamus' most controversial quatrains, both of which have been used in recent years to either confirm his gift of prophecy or repudiate it. First, Century X, Quatrain 72:

In the year 1999, and seven months,
from the sky will come the great King of Terror.
He will bring back to life the great king of the Mongols.
Before and after War reigns happily.

It can be argued that the great King of Terror is Osama Bin Laden, and that his boldest act of terror did indeed come from the sky in the kamikaze attack with airplanes on September 11 (the seventh month according to the Julian calendar that was in use when Nostradamus wrote his prophecies). But that was in 2001, not 1999. The rest of the quatrain is a stretch, but fits. Bin Laden did revive the barbarism of the Mongols and war in the Middle East – particularly in Iraq – preceded and succeeded the act.

Even more applicable – but oddly ignored by most interpreters in the wake of 9/11 – is Century I, Quatrain 87:

Earthshaking fire from the centre of the earth
will cause tremors around the New City.
Two great rocks will war for a long time,
then Arethusa will redden a new river.

The "earthshaking fire" could well refer to the two planes that crashed into each of the twin towers of the World Trade Center (*"centre of the earth"*). In the second line, the French words "au tour" are translated as "around," but "tour" is also the French word for "tower." "New City" is clearly "New York City." The third line could apply to the long-running War on Terror and Arethusa could be construed as an anagram for "The USA," which seeks retribution in blood (reddens a new river).

Or … maybe it has nothing to do with September 11. That's the frustrating thing about Nostradamus. In many cases, we see what we want to see in his prophecies. None of his verses are definitive.

Still, that hasn't stopped scores of contemporary pseudo-historians from dissecting, analyzing and embellishing the prophecies – especially those that conjure apocalyptic images of war, famine, pestilence and holocaust – for the primary purpose of turning a profit, even if it means alarming an impressionable audience.

There have been countless books written about Nostradamus. An Amazon search of his name alone produces approximately 1,457 results – everything from *Nostradamus for Dummies* to *Nostradamus Encyclopaedia*.

One of his most persistent biographers and interpreters is John Hogue, who actually looks like a direct descendant of the seer. His list of credits includes *Nostradamus: The Complete Prophecies*,

Nostradamus: The New Millennium, Nostradamus: A Life and Myth, The Essential Nostradamus for the 21st Century, and so on and so forth. Can you say obsession?

Hogue even took a stab at interpreting St. Malachy's Prophecies of the Popes. When the author isn't recycling the Centuries in print, he's hyping the hell out of the same overworked quatrains on a seemingly endless series of apocalypse-themed programs on the History Channel, repeated ad nauseum. These have included *The Lost Book of Nostradamus, The Nostradamus Effect,* and *Nostradamus 2012.*

For all their purported significance, the alleged apocalyptic quatrains of Nostradamus could apply to any war – major or minor. Yet in the hands of merchants of menace like Hogue, Century I, Quatrain 16 is seen as a prediction of World War III:

> *A scythe joined with a pond in Sagittarius*
> *at its highest ascendant.*
> *Plague, famine, death from military hands;*
> *the century approaches its renewal.*

And then there's the specious speculation surrounding Nostradamus's identification of the third (after Napoleon and Hitler) and final Antichrist. The consensus – based on Century II, Quatrain 29 – is that the future's biggest boogeyman will originate from Asia or the Middle East:

> *The man from the East will come out of his seat*
> *and will cross the Apennines to see France.*
> *He will cross through the sky, the seas and the snows*
> *and he will strike everyone with his rod.*

Others believe that Nostradamus provided the culprit's name in an anagram in Century II, Quatrain 62:

Mabus will then soon die and there will come
A dreadful destruction of people and animals.
Suddenly vengeance will be revealed,
A hundred hands, thirst and hunger, when the comet will pass.

Really?

As for the *piece de resistance*, a prediction from Nostradamus about the end of the world, the best one can come up with is Century X, Quatrain 74:

The year of the great seventh number accomplished,
it will appear at the time of the games of slaughter,
Not far from the age of the great millennium,
when the dead will come out of their graves.

As with all things potentially profitable, the Nostradamus phenomenon even went Hollywood. The first film to exploit his mystique was a 1957 B-movie called *The Man Without A Body* in which the seer's head is unearthed and reanimated for the purpose of a brain transplant – which makes about as much sense as one of Nostradamus' more obscure quatrains.

In 1981, the documentary *The Man Who Saw Tomorrow* kick-started the present Nostradamus craze into high gear. Presented and narrated by the late Orson Welles, the film sought to titillate audiences by illustrating the seer's life and predictions with dramatized scenes, stock footage and various television clips. Apparently, the project simply represented a payday for Mr. Welles as he publicly distanced himself from its central thesis – that Nostradamus was indeed a prophet. In fact, during a guest appearance on the *Merv Griffin Show* shortly after the film's release, Welles demurred: "One might as well make predictions based on random passages from the phone book."

Clearly, the oracle's best cinematic moment was in the 1994 biographic film *Nostradamus*, which focused on his life, loves and pursuit of enlightenment instead of sensationalizing his prophecies. However, despite its prestigious production values, the film hardly made a dent at the box office, no doubt because audiences preferred apocalyptic visions to contemplative costume drama.

No doubt about it, Nostradamus has become a worldwide, doomsday superstar – more famous in our era than he ever was in his own time. And in all likelihood, that fame will endure as long as there are those devoted to profiting from his legacy.

The supreme irony, of course, is that while others have made millions doing so, Nostradamus never saw dime one from the enterprise because he had the misfortune of dying several hundred years before the age of mass media. Who could have predicted that? Apparently not Nostradamus.

CHAPTER 5

The Mighty Cayce Has Struck Out

"Hey now, hey now, don't dream it's over." –Neil Finn (recorded by Crowded House)

ACCORDING TO WEBSTER'S Dictionary, the definitions of a prophet are "one who utters divinely inspired revelations," "one gifted with more than ordinary spiritual and moral insight," "one who foretells future events," and "an effective or leading spokesman for a cause, doctrine or group."

If those are the criteria, then Edgar Cayce certainly seemed to fit the bill. Dubbed "The Sleeping Prophet" because his revelations were delivered while in a trance-like state, Cayce is seen by many as the father of the New Age movement for reasons that will become apparent shortly. He has also become a hot, posthumous commodity for legions of Doomsday enthusiasts eager to capitalize on his apocalyptic visions. We'll address both aspects of his notoriety. But first, a little background …

Edgar Cayce was born on March 18, 1877 on a farm near Beverly, Kentucky. Financially strapped, his family could only afford to support his education up to the ninth grade at which time Edgar was forced to seek whatever employment was available. In the meantime, he drew spiritual comfort from his association with the Disciples of Christ. An avid churchgoer, he taught Sunday school, helped recruit missionaries and reportedly read the entire Bible once every year for the rest of his life.

At the age of 22, Cayce joined his father in selling insurance, but that vocation was short-lived as he developed severe laryngitis that rendered him speechless. Unemployed, he lived with his parents for the better part of a year before deciding to become a photographer.

Shortly thereafter, his life took an unusual turn when a traveling hypnotist arrived at the local Opera House, heard about Edgar's condition and offered to cure him of his vocal affliction onstage before an audience. With nothing to lose, Cayce accepted the offer and was placed in a trance. While under hypnosis, Edgar was able to talk – but lost his voice again once awakened.

He then turned to another hypnotist named Al Layne, who asked Cayce to describe both the nature of his ailment and how it could be cured while in a trance. Cayce did so, but not in the first person singular. Instead, he declared how "we" lost our voice due to psychological paralysis. His suggested cure was to increase blood flow to his voice box. Layne repeated the suggestion and, allegedly, Cayce's face and the skin on his chest and throat flushed a bright red. Shortly thereafter, while still in a trance, Edgar announced that his treatment was over. When he woke, Edgar Cayce was speaking normally.

Thus was born the healing method of the trance voice, which Cayce used thereafter to help cure others of their various medical problems and to support himself and his family through voluntary donations.

It didn't take long for the newspapers to get wind of this miraculous process, and soon Cayce received offers from a number of "entrepreneurs" eager to profit from his apparent clairvoyant abilities. Reluctantly, he obliged a few with readings, but soon discovered that his abilities were unsuccessfully when used for profit-making purposes. Not only did it weigh on his conscience, but it also made him physically and mentally weak. Ultimately, he decided to use his talent to help the sick.

Then, in 1923, while in an alleged trance, giving a reading for a wealthy printer named Arthur Lammers, Cayce reportedly spoke at length about reincarnation and revealed Lammers' past lives. When he awoke and was told what had been recorded, Cayce claimed that he could not have done any such thing because, as a devout Christian, he did not believe in reincarnation. However, Lammers managed to convince Cayce that he had indeed spoken of these things, using the first person plural trance voice of "we." It was then that Cayce came to the conclusion that the unconscious mind was a conduit for information to which the conscious mind was not privy – and he accepted his calling as a professional psychic.

In 1925, that trance voice instructed Cayce to move to Virginia Beach, Virginia where, assisted by a modest staff of employees and volunteers, he began giving readings on a regular basis.

Within four years, he also established a hospital with the sponsorship of Morton Blumenthal, a wealthy benefactor. Unlike other hospitals, however, this one prescribed holistic treatments that were considered unconventional at the time including poultices, folk remedies, osteopathic adjustment, colonic irrigation and electric medicine.

Over the next decade, Cayce performed thousands of psychic readings. His method consisted of lying down and entering a trance state – thus the moniker "The Sleeping Prophet" – and given his subjects' questions from a member of his staff. For the most part, the answers focused on the subject's health, but often pertained to mental or spiritual well-being, business advice, dream interpretations and past lives.

The deeper Cayce immersed himself in this routine, the more his belief system veered toward the occult and esoteric. For example, he believed in karma and accepted the pseudo-science of astrology based on the notion that human souls exist on other planets in between incarnations. He also placed credence in extrasensory perception, not to mention astral projection and the ability to see auras.

While in various trances, Cayce was not content to stick to crackpot medical advice, but also dispensed crackpot predictions of future events. In 1924, he predicted a stock market crash after a long bull market. It took five years for that forecast to come true and, in hindsight, was not a particular remarkable prediction. Any economist worth his salt knew that the financial joy ride of the Roaring 20's would have to come to a screeching halt. And numerous pundits over the last 80 years have made similar predictions that were eventually proven right in the wake of the dot.com and real estate bubbles.

In 1934, Cayce predicted that Adolf Hitler would rise to great power in Germany – a pretty educated guess considering Hitler became Chancellor of Deutschland in January 1933. In 1935, he added that Hitler would remain in power until he was deposed by "an overthrow or an outside war." Another safe bet.

Cayce's predictions about World War II were also hardly startling. He foresaw America's eventual participation in the conflict (another eventuality) and, in 1943, vaguely predicted there would soon be a "decisive" battle. Was he referring to the clash of Nazi and Russian tanks on the eastern front? D-Day on June 6, 1944? The Battle of the Bulge? Men in trances rarely elaborate.

Cayce is credited with accurately foreseeing the deaths of Franklin Roosevelt and John F. Kennedy by merely predicting in 1939 that "two American presidents would die while in office." He never gave a specific time frame on that one. But given the fact that Roosevelt ran for an unprecedented third and fourth terms and was confined to a wheelchair with a paralytic illness, it's a wonder that calculation didn't come true sooner than within 24 years.

But where Cayce really struck out – so far – were in his predictions of events beyond his lifetime. For example, he predicted that a "new land" would appear off the East Coast of the United States in 1968 or 1969 and would actually be part of the lost continent of Atlantis. The only Atlantis that emerged was the man-made resort on Paradise Island in the Bahamas, established in 1997.

He also predicted that by late 2001, archeologists would discover a great chamber beneath the Sphinx by the Pyramid of Gaza in Egypt. There, Cayce foretold, they would find a "magical library" containing proof of Atlantis' existence. There were excavations undertaken at Giza from 1988-1991, but nothing remotely related to the Lost Continent was uncovered.

We'll give Cayce points for accurately predicting the collapse of communism in the Soviet Union – although Vladimir Putin may have something to say about the reestablishment of totalitarianism in Russia before all is said and done.

Cayce also foresaw the rise of technology – like every visionary from Leonardo DaVinci to Jules Verne and H.G. Wells.

One of Cayce's more controversial predictions was that the Earth's poles would shift around the year 2000. The implication was that this would have a significant and catastrophic effect on the planet's climate. His defenders claim that NASA confirmed a change in the Earth's gravitational field in 1998 that moved the magnetic poles closer together. But there is no such official report and in the absence of a related earth-shattering event, the deadline has been extended to – guess when – 2012.

Last but not least, Cayce predicted that Christ would return to Earth in 1998 and the battle of Armageddon would occur in 1999. Wrong again.

Edgar Cayce gained national prominence in 1943 as the subject of an article in *Coronet* magazine entitled, "Miracle Man of Virginia Beach." By then, however, his schedule of eight readings per day had taken a toll on his own health, leaving him emotionally drained and severely fatigued. He began to limit his workload to just two readings a day, but by then it was too late.

Cayce suffered a stroke and died on January 3, 1945, yet lives on in the form of the Association for Enlightenment and Research (A.R.E.), a "not for profit organization founded in 1931 ... to research and explore transpersonal subjects ..." Besides its headquarters in Virginia Beach, A.R.E. also maintains regional headquarters in Houston and Edgar Cayce Centers in 37 countries. In addition to holistic remedies, the Association's Web site also offers Edgar Cayce-related merchandise including DVDs, CDs and T-shirts.

Cayce also lives on as the posthumous godfather of the New Age movement – which had its roots in the 18th and 19th centuries, but truly blossomed in the aftermath of the consciousness-expanding 1960's – and as the subject of numerous books. Like Nostradamus before him, the Sleeping Prophet has evolved into the Sleeping Cash Cow for various biographers.

In 1950, Cayce's alleged psychic abilities were chronicled in Gina Cerminara's book, *Many Mansions: The Edgar Cayce Story on Reincarnation* (Signet). But Cayce's notoriety soared more than twenty years after his death with the release of author Jess Stearn's biography, *The Sleeping Prophet: The Life and Work of Edgar Cayce* (Bantam Books, 1967). Coming on the heels of Ruth Montgomery's bestseller about Jeane Dixon (*A Gift of Prophecy*), *The Sleeping Prophet* sold millions of copies and prompted a less successful sequel entitled: *A Prophet In His Own Country: The Story of the Young Edgar Cayce* (1974). Numerous other books about Cayce and his visions about everything from Atlantis to the Dead Sea Scrolls to the healing properties of colors, stones and crystals followed over the years.

Not surprisingly, Cayce's support of alternative medicine has raised many an eyebrow and dismissive charges of outright quackery. Cayce's minions claim that as a healer he had a success rate of more than 85 percent, but that has never been independently verified.

What's more, his unconventional religious beliefs, melding the principles of various sects under the banner of "Oneness," have not won Cayce many converts among conservative Christians.

And in regard to his alleged gift of communing with the spirit world, critics have suggested that Cayce was merely an attention seeker with an overactive imagination. As author Michael Shermer pointed out in *Why People Believe Weird Things* (2002), Cayce "acquired his knowledge through voracious reading and from this he wove elaborate tales … Cayce was fantasy-prone from his youth, often talking to angels and receiving visions of his dead grandfather."

Famed illusionist and skeptic James (the Amazing) Randi also noted that "Cayce was fond of expressions like 'I feel that' and 'perhaps'

– qualifying words used to avoid positive declarations."

Yet despite these detractors, Edgar Cayce reputation among doomsday devotees remains relatively untarnished. He is still viewed by many wishful thinkers as a latter day seer. And as long as that's the case, it is likely that the exploitation of his tenuous prophecies will continue.

But in the humble opinion of this doubting Thomas – we should let sleeping prophets lie.

CHAPTER **6**

The Prime of Ms. Jeane Dixon

"Don't ever prophesy; for if you prophesy wrong, nobody will forget it; and if you prophesy right, nobody will remember it."
-- Josh Billings

THEY DUBBED IT the Swinging Sixties – an era of conflict, chaos, revolution, uncertainty, political and social upheaval – all rolled into one. But with war raging in Southeast Asia, U.S. urban ghettoes burning, political assassination becoming the new American national pastime, the Woodstock generation literally going to pot, and the Four Horsemen of the Apocalypse leading the British musical invasion, they might as well have called it the "Eve of Destruction."

Like another popular song of the time proclaimed, it was the dawning of the Age of Aquarius – and the dawning of the age of the curious. The New Age movement was starting to gain traction and there was considerable interest in all things mystical. The world was ripe and ready for a new type of prophet to arise – one accompanied and empowered by media hype and the sheer gullibility of the impressionable masses. Only this time, the prophet was a prophetess and her name was Jeane Dixon.

She was born Lydia Emma Pinckert in Medford, Wisconsin in 19 …

Well, that's the thing – Dixon often claimed she was born in 1918 and even had that birth date on her passport. But that seemed highly unlikely when it later came to light that she was first married in 1928 (at the age of 10?) to a Swiss immigrant named Charles Zuercher, whom she divorced several years later. Once, under oath in a deposition, Dixon admitted to being born in 1910. However, official records unearthed in the course of an investigation by the *National Observer* confirmed that she was actually born in *1904*. While it's not unusual for some people in the public eye to lie about their age, a 14-year disparity seems to have abused the privilege and only reflected unflatteringly on Dixon's veracity.

Although she hailed from the Land of Lakes, Dixon was raised in Missouri and Southern California, where her father owned and operated an automobile dealership. Not surprisingly, Lydia went on to marry a car dealer – James Dixon – in 1939 with whom she would remain married without children until his death in 1984. In time, the Dixons moved to Washington, D.C. where James ran a lucrative real estate firm. Lydia, now known as Jeane, worked with her husband for a number of years and even served as the company's Secretary-Treasurer.

Jeane Dixon claimed that, as a young girl, she had her palm read by a "gypsy" who predicted a career as a famous seer and advisor to men in power. Not only that, but the fortuneteller also bestowed her with a gift – her very own crystal ball. If true, the encounter culminated in a self-fulfilling prophecy.

Later, as the wife of an affluent Washingtonian, Dixon became a member of the local social scene. She entertained servicemen and a number of dignitaries during World War II with her fortune-telling and gradually cultivated a reputation for forecasting events such as the airplane crash that claimed the life of Hollywood star Carole Lombard and the assassination of Mahatma Gandhi. Corroboration of these predictions often came from influential personal friends and led to private readings for none other than President Franklin Delano Roosevelt in 1944 and 1945.

Dixon's method of divining the future was through the aforementioned crystal ball, as well as the occasional revelation, vision, oracular dream and by picking up someone's "vibrations" through a handshake.

Throughout the late 1940's and early 1950's, she continued to give readings at local parties, and in 1956 achieved a modicum of notoriety beyond the Beltway when *Parade* magazine reported "for the 1960 election, Mrs. Dixon thinks it will be dominated by labor and won by a Democrat. But he will be assassinated or die in office, 'though not necessarily in his first term.'" Although then-Senator John F. Kennedy was not identified by name, Dixon did describe the doomed future president as "young, tall, and blue-eyed, with a shock of thick brown hair." Supposedly, she reiterated this prediction on many subsequent occasions and with more frequency in the days leading up to November 22, 1963.

The unfortunate fulfillment of this forecast proved to be a game changer for the Divine Ms. D and led to the publication of her biography, *A Gift of Prophecy,* by journalist Ruth Montgomery in 1965. The book was a huge *New York Times* bestseller, moving three million copies worldwide in its initial printings, earning Dixon her own syndicated newspaper column and establishing her as the Ezekiel of her time.

With a handful of sources to back her claims, Montgomery credited the prophetess with not only predicting JFK's assassination seven years before it happened, but also the Chinese communist revolution in 1949, Sputnik in 1957 and the death of Marilyn Monroe in 1962.

So much for the accurate stuff. Unfortunately, the book required a chapter devoted to Jeane Dixon's future forecasts which, in hindsight, marked the beginning of her undoing as a credible, modern-day Oracle of Delphi. Among her memorable misses:

- *"Russia will be the first nation to put a man on the moon."*
- *"Our two biggest headaches will be the racial problem and Red China. Through the latter's subversion and meddling in the racial strife, numerous African and Asian nations will turn against us and provoke a world war in the decade of the 1980's."*

- Saw continued success for the Beatles, *"though one of them would 'unfortunately branch out from the team before long, and later regret it,'"* and foresaw no *"violent death for any of the four entertainers."*
- *"Red China will invade Russian territory, but this will be a border skirmish and will not ignite the later war to come, in which Red China will wage 'germ warfare.' In this period late in the century the Davis Straits will become an American 'life line.'"*
- A Middle Eastern child whose birth she witnessed in a vision on February 5, 1962 *"will unite all warring creeds and sects into one all-embracing faith. Mankind will begin to feel the great force of this man about 1980, and his power 'will grow mightily' until 1999, when there will be 'peace on earth to all men of good will.'"*

Nevertheless, these misses had no immediate effect on Dixon's status as America's prophet laureate. After all, it took decades for most of them to be proven wrong.

Instead of quitting while she was somewhat ahead, however, Dixon felt compelled to duplicate the success of *A Gift of Prophecy* by releasing 1969's *My Life and Prophecies* (as told to Rene Noorbergen). In the follow-up book, she not only explained her modus operandi in greater detail, but also took credit for predicting the assassinations of Martin Luther King and Robert F. Kennedy and issued all sorts of predictions for the immediate and long-range future. The only thing Mrs. Dixon didn't predict was how poorly her new predictions would fare.

If *A Gift of Prophecy* established Jeane Dixon's reputation as a soothsayer, *My Life and Prophecies* all but demolished it. Most embarrassing was a prediction entitled "New Profession for Bishop Pike," in which she forecast that the clergyman would find success in a new career. After the book was printed and on the eve of its release, Bishop Pike perished in the Judean desert.

Other inaccurate predictions included:

- Ethel Kennedy, Robert F. Kennedy's widow, would remarry. She never did.
- A comet would hit Earth in the 1980s. Didn't happen.
- The first woman president of the United States would be elected ("… I feel it will surely be in the 1980's."). Still waiting.
- The end of Castro was in sight. The Cuban dictator not only outlived Dixon, but is still in charge more than 40 years after the prediction was made.
- Richard Nixon would appoint five justices to the Supreme Court. Close but no cigar – Nixon picked four.

To make matters worse, these were just the latest in a series of miscalculations issued by Dixon between publication of *A Gift of Prophecy* and *My Life and Prophecies*. She also missed the mark when she predicted the marriage of First Daughter Lynda Bird Johnson to actor George Hamilton, whom she merely dated on a few occasions. And then there was the prediction that the Vietnam War would end in 1965 – Dixon was only off by 10 years.

On October 20, 1968, Dixon submitted a column containing the prediction that she saw "no marriage for Jackie (Kennedy) in the near future." The piece was withdrawn just in the nick of time when news came over the wire that Jacqueline had married Aristotle Onassis that very day.

Many began to wonder why Dixon's "gift" was suddenly so far afield. Did fame jinx her, ruining her ability to see clearly into the future? Is it any coincidence that her record was so uncanny when predictions were revealed *after the fact* and not nearly as accurate when shared with the public before the event? Her standard excuse was that her visions weren't wrong, she just occasionally "misinterpreted the symbols." But could there have been another fly in the ointment?

Dixon not only had a gift for prophesying, but also for pontificating. A devout Catholic (except for that ancient divorce she covered up for years) and a staunch conservative, Dixon was as opinionated as she was ethereal and saw the world through the prism of her crystal ball as black and white. Thus, many of her "predictions" in the Montgomery book were actually political broadsides against liberalism and what she believed was America's misguided international and domestic initiatives. For example:

> *"Our foreign policy should be motivated by the desire to protect American interests, rather than by 'some mysterious humanitarian ideal.' We should not try to make over European nations in our own image, but rather accept the differences and work with them."*

Elsewhere she stated: *"The President's [Lyndon Johnson] program for the Great Society will fail, because the channels are running in all directions and none of the ends are closed. His War on Poverty will also fail unless more spirituality is introduced into the program, because 'man does not live by bread alone, and it takes more than food and money to restore the dignity of man.'"* While one could argue that the Great Society did fail, one could also argue that this was more of a sanctimonious editorial than a prediction and one that any political pundit could have made.

Dixon's fatal flaw as a prognosticator was her tendency to formulate her mystical predictions through the filter of her personal political views and religious philosophy. In *My Life and Prophecies,* Dixon's crystal ball would tell her that Martin Luther King was an "unwitting tool of the Communists." She received "good vibrations" from political figures like Richard Nixon, Barry Goldwater and Ronald Reagan, but bemoaned the policies of liberal counterparts Lyndon Johnson, Robert Kennedy and George McGovern. She even took a swipe at baby boomers – who she evidently assumed were all pot-smoking, free-lovin', antiestablishment hippies – when she predicted that the youth of the Woodstock generation "who neglect spiritual values will suffer untold misery." This, surely, was Dixon's Achilles heel – her failure to interpret her visions objectively.

Also damaging to Dixon's credibility later in her career were her frequent articles in the *National Star,* a supermarket tabloid that catered to sensationalism and yet the appropriate forum for her brand of daffy divination. Amidst predictions of when Elizabeth Taylor would remarry and which celebrity should guard against accident or injury, she would include more earth-shattering forecasts such as "an antibiotic-resistant strain of influenza" spreading across the globe – apparently unaware that antibiotics don't have an effect on viruses.

Despite her checkered record, Jeane Dixon appeared on numerous TV talk programs including the *David Susskind Show* (where she claimed that the Virgin Mary had told her that the United States needed to bomb Russian ships in the Black Sea), the *Merv Griffin Show* and the *Dick Cavett Show*. She was also a fixture on the lecture circuit and established a widely syndicated astrological newspaper column – after admitting years earlier that she didn't know a thing about astrology.

But the most controversial of Dixon's predictions naturally involved her convoluted scenario for the End Times. In *A Gift of Prophecy*, she came to the conclusion that the as-yet-to-be-revealed Third Secret of Fatima foretold the assassination of a Pope and the end of the papacy. When the Third Secret was finally revealed, it was actually concerned with the future persecution of the Catholic Church. Meanwhile, in *My Life and Prophecies*, Dixon did a complete about face regarding the child born in the Middle East on February 4, 1962 whom she had previously pegged as the New Messiah. He now took on a more sinister role and was – in fact – the Antichrist himself. Talk about a woman's prerogative to change her mind.

Quoting the Book of Revelation, Dixon painted an apocalyptic picture similar to that of other false prophets before and after her – that of a charismatic political and spiritual leader who, like the Pied Piper, would beguile the world, gaining dominion over all mankind and leading souls astray as a prelude to the glorious second coming of Jesus Christ. Somehow, in the midst of this grand deception, those dastardly Red Chinese would precipitate Armageddon. And how would this conflict end? As usual, Dixon's timing and rationality were off:

> "I have projected my quest for information into the year 2000 and see Chinese and Mongol troops invading the Middle East. I see devastating battles raging uncontrollably east of the Jordan River. It is a war of East against West. It will be an almost futile fight against an overwhelming foe – but the Lord will place Himself at the side of Israel, and great losses will be suffered by the Orientals … After the tide of battle has shifted, Israel will become one of the greatest miracles of all times, for the Israelites will then realize that it was God's intervention that brought about this ultimate victory, and they will finally accept Jesus Christ as the Son of God."

As for the fate of the Antichrist, Dixon was vaguely allegorical: *"I saw a great crowd follow him reverently as he walked up a long road. This marked the end of his rule. In awe and filled with blind adoration, they followed him, neglecting to listen to the inner voice of the Lord that called them to repent … I saw humanity arrive at the 'valley of decision,' a fork in the road, where the 'Child of the East' … made a sharp turn to the left … This moment marked the point of decision, for here everyone individually was given the choice of either veering to the left and following the child or going on, continuing to where the path became straight and narrow … the uncountable masses followed him in quiet adoration. I look ahead, and the vision dissolved into utter darkness and desolation that awaited them at the end of the road."*

Thus the expression, mumbo-jumbo.

Jeane Dixon met her maker on January 25, 1997 at the age of 92 … or was it 86 … 79? Whatever. And while it is easy to dismiss Jeane Dixon's delusional visions and credentials as a legitimate psychic, her influence on succeeding generations of would-be prophets and doomsday demagogues cannot be discounted.

Not only did she pave the way for countless imitators on- and offline, but she also pioneered the prevailing evangelical theory on how the End Times will eventually go down. And, if nothing else, she proved that one could make a lucrative living dispensing grossly inaccurate information to people with an insatiable appetite for awful forecasts about their own futures. Hers was a true American success story, for only here could a person with so little to offer in the way of true foresight go so far.

CHAPTER **7**

Hollywood Babble On

"No one ever went broke underestimating the intelligence of the American public." – Henry Louis Mencken

WHO IN THEIR right mind would consider the end of the world entertainment? Movie producers, of course! And not just the studio suits, but also millions of filmgoers willing to fork over their hard-earned cash for tickets to the spectacle. In fact, more doomsday profits have been pocketed from Hollywood blockbusters and B-movies than from any other medium.

Actually, the first significant apocalyptic "cinematic" experience wasn't a film at all, but the Mercury Theatre's infamous 1938 radio production of H.G. Wells' *War of the Worlds*. Aired on Halloween and preceded by a disclaimer, the event nonetheless caused a panic among listeners who believed they were hearing a real emergency in which Martians had landed in New Jersey (of all places) and were rampaging the countryside, annihilating everything in their path. The incident proved to be wunderkind Orson Welles' ticket to Tinseltown and immortality as a tortured genius auteur. It also gave the entertainment industry a clue as to how to spin Doomsday fears into box-office gold.

It wasn't long after the *War of the Worlds* broadcast and the actual holocaust of World War II that Hollywood truly got into the act. At first, apocalyptic scenarios were the stuff of bad, mediocre or great science fiction. One early purveyor of the third kind was George Pal, producer of such classics as *When Worlds Collide (1951)*, *War of the Worlds (1953)* and *The Time Machine (1960)*.

In *When Worlds Collide,* an astronomer discovers that a "star" named Bellus is on a collision course with Earth and tries to convince the United Nations to build spacecrafts that will shuttle a handful of survivors to Zyra, an Earth-like planet orbiting the wayward constellation where mankind can sustain itself. His pleas fall on deaf ears until a group of wealthy humanitarians step in to fund the project. As Bellus neared its target, audiences were offered the startling image of Times Square being engulfed by a tsunami, one of several scenes that earned the film an Academy Award for Special Effects.

Pal's screen version of *War of the Worlds* also had its share of eye-popping – for its time – apocalyptic effects as Martian war machines laid waste to Los Angeles and other environs with disintegrator rays. And although *The Time Machine* (which Pal also directed) envisioned a future world populated by the gentle and passive Eloi and the cannibalistic, subterranean Morlocks, it included a scene set in 1966 in which nuclear war ends civilization as we know it for more than 800,000 years.

Perhaps taking his cue from George Pal, producer Irwin Allen established himself as the "Master of Disaster" in the 1960's and 70's with movies such as 1961's *Voyage To The Bottom of the Sea,* a global warming film before anyone heard the phrase "global warming."

In the film, a meteor shower has pierced the Van Allen radiation belt – a fancier name for the ozone layer – and effectively set it on fire, causing temperatures to rise precipitously around the globe and threatening all life on the planet. Only a state-of-the-art submarine manned by Walter Pigeon, Peter Lorre and Frankie Avalon and armed with nuclear missiles can extinguish the fire and put the ecology back in balance before it's too late.

As wacky as that now sounds, the film was a major hit, spawned a television series, and gave Allen the green light to produce other blockbuster disaster films including *The Poseidon Adventure* (1972) and *The Towering Inferno* (1974), the latter of which now plays as an unsettling reminder of the September 11th World Trade Center tragedy.

Pioneers though they were, George Pal and Irwin Allen were just a few of the many motion picture impresarios who, over the last 70 years or so, have produced countless films dealing in some way with the end of the world – some morbidly entertaining, some surprisingly thought-provoking, and some just plain cockamamie.

However, it wasn't until the Atomic Age of the 1950's that Hollywood realized that there were big bucks to be made cranking out B-movies that capitalized on Cold War fears. Not only did nuclear fission lead to mutants and monsters, it also opened a Pandora's box of valid concerns about the possibility of a third world war. Whereas early ruminations on that subject – in movies such as *Five* (1955) and *The World, The Flesh and the Devil* (1959) – stuck to the consequences of an atomic war, later films sought to make the case for nuclear disarmament once it was clear that the McCarthy era was over and it was safe for filmmakers to take such a "controversial" position.

One of the most compelling examples of a ban-the-bomb movie came in 1960 with the release of director Stanley Kramer's *On The Beach*. Based on a novel by Nevil Chute, the film focused on the doomed last survivors of a nuclear holocaust living or stationed in Australia, waiting for the radioactivity to reach them. One of the most chilling scenes comes at the finale of the film when, to a stirring rendition of the tune *Waltzing Matilda*, we see abandoned city streets once teeming with humanity and zoom in on a powerful message left on a sagging streamer, the apparent remnant of a revival meeting: "There is still time … Brother."

Those nuclear Armageddon fears – fueled to an extent by the real threat posed by the Cuban Missile Crisis in 1962 – were subsequently well represented on the screen by such films as *Ladybug, Ladybug* (1963); *Fail Safe (1964); The Bedford Incident (1965)*; and Stanley Kubrick's black comedy *Dr. Strangelove: Or How I Learned To Stop*

Worrying and Love the Bomb (1964), which provided the iconic image of Slim Pickens riding a nuclear bomb like a bucking bronco all the way down to its Soviet target.

And, of course, who could forget the memorable twist ending to the *Planet of the Apes* (1968) when stranded astronaut Charlton Heston stumbles upon the wreckage of the Statue of Liberty on a desolate beach and realizes he's back on Earth many years in the future following a nuclear holocaust. The film's sequel, *Beneath the Planet of the Apes* (1970) elaborated on the Armageddon theme with underground mutants who have literally learned to stop worrying and love the bomb.

And it wasn't just Hollywood cashing in on the craze. Foreign studios and audiences were also in tune to the commercial possibilities of the nuclear age. In the U.K.-produced *The Day the Earth Caught Fire* (1961), it is learned that atomic testing has shifted the Earth's axis and the planet is now heading toward the sun. Although that scenario now seems preposterous based on modern science, this well-acted and thought-provoking film chillingly depicted the collapse of social order in the wake of a manmade calamity.

There was also *La Jetée* (1962), a haunting 28-minute French film told in black and white still photos that depicted a post-nuclear war experiment in time travel intended to alter the past. Although the film was about the power and mystery of memory with romantic overtones – not a political or moral statement about the possible consequences of nuclear proliferation – it is worth mentioning as the source or inspiration for later pre- and post-apocalyptic films such as *Twelve Monkeys* and *The Terminator*.

Even the plots of several James Bond adventures – notably *The Spy Who Loved Me* (1977) and *Moonraker* (1979) – utilized the threat of global extinction via nuclear confrontation or germ warfare to raise the emotional stakes, infuse some suspense and lure fans into theatres.

In 1977, the fledgling Australian film industry got a boost with director Peter Weir's apocalyptically-themed *The Last Wave*. American actor Richard Chamberlain starred as an Aussie attorney assigned to defend an aborigine accused of murder, only to discover that he himself has a mystical connection to the tribe in a previous life and a repressed gift of clairvoyance. Weird weather phenomena plague the country and ominous visions plague the attorney until a startling final scene puts everything in stark context.

But whereas cinema once focused serious attention on the impending menace of nuclear war and natural disaster, it gradually gravitated more toward religiously based end-times speculation. A prime example is *The Omen* series. Following in the highly successful footsteps of *Rosemary's Baby (1968)*, in which the son of Satan is born into the modern world, *The Omen* expanded on the scenario to chilling yet dubious effect.

The film introduced a five-year-old Antichrist named Damien Thorn protected by evil disciples and seemingly invincible as those who stand in his way on the path to maturity and global domination are dispatched in graphically gory fashion by unseen, demonic forces. Preying on ancient fears of the devil and the public's morbid fascination with stylistic violence, the producers certainly gave audiences their money's worth while propagating the Armageddon theories of certain evangelicals as evidenced by a prophetic poem that figures prominently in the film:

When the Jews return to Zion,
and a comet rips the sky,
and the Holy Roman Empire rises,
then you and I must die.

From the eternal sea he rises,
building armies on either shore,
turning man against his brother,
till man exists no more.

Neither Nostradamus nor Old Mother Shipton could've penned it better. However, these verses are not Biblical as the film would have you believe, but instead the invention of screenwriter David Seltzer based on common liberal interpretations of the Book of Revelation and other scriptures.

Slickly produced (at a mere $2.5 million) and grimly entertaining, *The Omen* became one of the hit films of 1976, grossing about $61 million domestically. Regrettably, its success led to two inferior sequels, *Damien-Omen II* and *The Final Conflict*, which were met with critical disdain and diminishing box office returns. Nevertheless, *The Omen* trilogy also spawned a 1991 TV movie (*Omen IV: The Awakening*) and novelizations, and the original film was remade in 2006, grossing $119.6 million worldwide on a $25 million budget.

Similar end-times films in which mankind must contend with Satanic forces have tested the box-office waters over the intervening years, but none with the same impact as *The Omen*. For example, in *End of Days* (1999) the only thing preventing the Prince of Darkness (in the guise of Gabriel Byrne) from impregnating his would-be baby mama is Arnold Schwarzenegger, a New York City cop with a thick Austrian accent. Unfortunately, Jesus *does not* have a cameo in the film declaring, "I'll be back." Despite its timely release on the cusp of the millennium, the film underperformed at the box-office and may have been one of the reasons Schwarzenegger decided to take a stab at politics.

1999 was also the year that the evangelical movement went Hollywood with its own rip-off of *The Omen* entitled *The Omega Code* (1999). Funded in part by the Trinity Broadcasting Network, the film chronicled the rise of the Antichrist (played by British-born actor Michael York), taking melodramatic license with Book of Revelation prophecy to unintentionally comic lengths. Despite heavy marketing to the evangelical community, the $7.6 million production only mustered $12.6 million worth of B.O. But that didn't prevent its producers from unleashing a sequel, *Meggido: The Omega Code 2* (2001), which cost them $22 million to make and grossed a mere $6 million.

There was also a lot of apocalyptic gibberish in the incomprehensible 1988 thriller *The Seventh Sign*, starring Demi Moore as a pregnant woman whose unborn child holds the key to mankind's salvation as signs of the Apocalypse unfold around her. But that didn't fly with audiences, either. And now that the dreaded Millennium has passed, the well has pretty much run dry on the psycho-biblical-babble genre.

Which is not to say that apocalyptic films based on religious beliefs cannot engage the intellect and raise profound questions. Hardly a love letter to evangelism, 1991's *The Rapture* tells the absorbing tale of a promiscuous woman, played by Mimi Rogers, who suddenly finds herself fascinated with a sect that warns her that the Rapture is about to occur. Disillusioned with her dead-end libidinous lifestyle, she converts to born-again Christianity, marries and has a daughter. When her husband becomes a victim of a workplace rampage, she goes to extreme measures to hasten the day of reckoning only to question her faith when the Rapture actually *does* occur, preferring eternity in Limbo to kowtowing to a fickle God. Written and directed by Michael Tolkin, this is arguably the best end-times movie ever.

Then again, there's a special place in DVD hell for "been there, done that" doomsday movies like 1980's *Meteor*, starring Sean Connery and Natalie Wood. A feeble recycling of *When Worlds Collide*, it too offered the spectacle of a heavenly body on a collision course with planet Earth, but this time with some of the cheesiest special effects this side of Ed Wood and the SyFy Channel. Conveniently, the lumbering space rock in question – which looks as if it is hurtling at a speed of 2 miles per hour – eventually lands in midtown Manhattan where, of course, our hero and his heroine happen to be stationed. The big bad meteor wasn't the only thing that fell to Earth – box-office receipts crashed and burned as well.

If meteors as weapons of mass destruction didn't appeal to moviegoers, asteroids and comets fared much better with the release of *Deep Impact* and the inexplicable-titled *Armageddon* in 1998. Of the two competing, big-budget blockbusters, *Deep Impact* (certainly not to be confused with *Deep Throat*) was the most plausible, offering a more reflective approach to the proceedings along with some striking CGI images – like a 1000-foot high tsunami engulfing New York City (yet another homage to *When Worlds Collide*) – and some unintentional amusing ones such as a man reading a newspaper in Washington Square Park, oddly oblivious to the huge wave that will momentarily wipe him out. It also raised the extinction level event stakes by featuring *two* deadly asteroids, thus allowing one to hit Earth and wreak considerable havoc and the other one to be spectacularly destroyed.

Armageddon, on the other hand, provided some cheap thrills like the destruction of Paris (the target is always a major, high-populated tourist attraction), but was saddled with a preposterous plot typical of the hyperactive, low-brow Joe Simpson-Jerry Bruckheimer productions of the 90's. Guess which movie made the most money at the box office?

The latter featured action hero Bruce Willis and a "lovable" group of booze-guzzling, redneck oil riggers and parole jumpers enlisted by NASA to rocket into space, land on a moving asteroid, drill a hole, deposit a nuclear device and blow the sucker to smithereens. Even the title of the film is boneheaded. Armageddon – as we all know – is the last, decisive war between good and evil. What that has to do with a mission to destroy a killer asteroid is a mystery. But who cares? They could have called it *Ishtar II* and it still would have cleaned up at the box office.

Although the Cold War officially ended in the late 1980's, nuclear anxiety was still on the minds of the makers of 1988's *Miracle Mile*, in which an L.A. couple's planned first date is interrupted by a twist of fate – a wrong-number phone call that tips off the main protagonist to an impending nuclear attack. The couple has 50 minutes to find each other and flee the city before all hell breaks loose, but instead find themselves trapped in a nightmarish urban deathtrap as news of the attack – and panic – starts to spread.

Then there's *The Terminator* franchise. The original film released in 1984, directed by James Cameron and starring Arnold Schwarzenegger as a killer cyborg, borrowed a concept from the aforementioned *La*

Jetée – that of time travel for the purpose of altering history. In this case, the terminator's mission is to eliminate mankind's future savior and thus ensure the takeover of the planet by the machines that triggered a nuclear holocaust. The wildly unanticipated success of *The Terminator* led to several equally popular sequels that expanded the series' mythology and even spawned the television series, *The Sarah Connor Chronicles*. Originally, "Judgment Day" was scheduled for August 29, 1997, but kept being postponed as the legacy spilled over into the 21st century.

Time out for a trivia question: Which role in various incarnations was shared by actors Vincent Price, Charlton Heston and Will Smith?

Answer: That would be the main protagonist in three separate movie versions of Richard Matheson's 1954 novel *I Am Legend*. Price got the ball rolling with his portrayal of the sole immune survivor of a global virus that turned others into vampire zombies in the Italian-made 1964 B-movie, *The Last Man On Earth*, an unacknowledged precursor to the legendary *Night of the Living Dead*. Only seven years later, Hollywood remade the film with Charlton Heston in the lead and called it *The Omega Man*. Finally, in 2007, Will Smith's cache as a superstar raked in more than half a billion dollars in worldwide receipts with a film named after the book, but a pale imitation of the original novel.

In remaking *La Jetée* as the full-length *Twelve Monkeys* (1995), director Terry Gilliam substituted thermonuclear war with a global pandemic as the apocalyptic event of choice. Fortunately, pestilence merely brought death as there has been a tiresome epidemic of movie zombies as of late, ranging from the staggering masses of endless George A. Romero *Living Dead* sequels to the frenetic, Rage-infected predators of *28 Days Later*.

Of course the most spectacular Doomsday depictions tend to be those dealing with alien invasions or Mother Nature with PMS. Good examples of the former are Steven Spielberg's grim remake of *War of the Worlds* (2005) and Roland Emmerich's *Independence Day* (1996), which was essentially *WOTW* on steroids. A more frivolous example is Tim Burton's *Mars Attacks* (1995), which took a shockingly graphic trading card series from the 1960s and turned it into a star-studded but irrelevant satire and a major missed opportunity.

Speaking of producer/director Roland Emmerich, the German-born auteur has emerged as the George Pal of the 21st century. Irwin Allen may have been the Master of Disaster, but he was a piker compared to Emmerich whose disaster flicks *The Day After Tomorrow* (2004) and *2012* (2009) – along with *Independence Day* – are among the highest grossing films of all time (*see chart*).

The Day After Tomorrow gave the Apocalypse an ecological spin, blaming global warming for the near extinction of humanity in the wake of meteorological havoc. Released at the height of Al Gore idol worship, the theme resonated with audiences to the tune of $544 million at the box-office.

Meanwhile, *2012* is arguably the mother of all disaster movies – so far. Shamelessly exploiting Doomsday speculation surrounding the end of the Mayan calendar, the film is one overlong, mind-numbing CGI orgy of axis-shifting earthquakes, volcanoes and tsunamis – although the release of the film just three years before the predicted event doesn't give it much of a shelf life. In fact, come December 22, 2012, the movie will be more or less outdated. But by then, Emmerich and his Hollywood colleagues will probably find another cataclysm to titillate moviegoers in 3-D.

And if computer-generated depictions of mankind's extinction aren't your bag, there are movies that are less concerned with how the world will end than with how human beings will deal with it. Doomsday is greeted in a variety of ways in the acclaimed 1998 Canadian independent film, *Last Night*. The cause of Earth's demise at midnight (Eastern Standard Time) is not specified, but has something to do with the sun getting progressively brighter. Billions have known this day was coming for months and while some choose to go out with a bang (literally and figuratively), others settle for a whimper.

Assuming that the only thing more intriguing than an end-times movie is one that speculates on life *after* Doomsday, Hollywood has produced a substantial array of post-apocalyptic fare with mixed results. On the lucrative side, there is the Mad Max trilogy of the late 1970's and early 1980's starring Mel Gibson as a former highway patrolman turned frontier warrior helping settlers and other survivors ward off barbaric marauders. All three films in the series were worldwide box-office hits with the second, *The Road Warrior*, arguably one of the best action films ever made.

Perhaps with Mad Max in mind, former box office golden boy Kevin Costner produced and starred in not one, but two three-hour, big budget post-apocalyptic films – *Waterworld* and *The Postman*. Both were duds that demoted Costner from Hollywood's A-list.

More recently, audiences took a pass on the screen adaptation of Cormac McCarthy's bestselling, Pulitzer Prize-winning novel *The Road (2009)* starring Viggo Mortgensen as a man on a treacherous cross-country trek with his young son in the aftermath of an undisclosed holocaust. A tale of paternal love and the struggle for survival amid a bleak and desolate landscape, the film proved too grim and ponderous for audiences weaned on demolition derby car chases and gratuitous acts of violence.

Another bleak but intriguing vision of Doomsday can be found in *Melancholia* (2011), director Lars von Trier's psychological disaster/ family drama film in which another planet is on an unavoidable collision course with Earth. It's a thought-provoking, restrained meditation on annihilation (among other things) and the artistic polar opposite of *2012*.

Every few years Hollywood comes up with a new and entertaining way to end the world with a money-grubbing glee epitomized by Slim Pickens in *Dr. Strangelove*, riding that nuclear bomb like a buckin' bronco. And despite this disturbing trend, audiences can't seem to look away from this cinematic equivalent of a major train wreck – kind of like Lot's wife glancing back at Sodom and Gomorrah.

As the tagline for the original *The Last House on the Left* suggested: Keep telling yourself, it's only a movie. If moviegoers do that and keep things in context, I guess it's better to end the world in the fantasy world of film than in reality. Or at least that's how Hollywood sees it.

Ka-ching!

Top 10 Highest Grossing Doomsday/Post-Apocalyptic Movies

1. Independence Day (1996) - $817.4 million
2. 2012 (2009) - $769.7 million
3. War of the Worlds (2005) - $591.7 million
4. I Am Legend (2007) - $585.3 million
5. Armageddon (1998) - $553.7 million
6. The Day After Tomorrow (2004) - $544.3 million
7. Terminator 2: Judgment Day - $519.8 million
8. Terminator 3: Rise of the Machines (2003) - $433 million
9. Terminator Salvation (2009) - $371.4 million
10. Planet of the Apes (2001) - $362.2 million

Source: boxofficemojo.com

Will the Real Antichrist Please Stand Up?

"Scott Baio is the Antichrist!" – *Comedian Bobcat Goldthwaite*

EVERY LITERARY EPIC – whether it's *The Lord of the Rings, The Chronicles of Narnia* or *Harry Potter* – has one common plot element – a struggle between good and the forces of evil. There is always a main hero (the good) and a formidable villain (the bad and the ugly), a protagonist the reader can identify with and an antagonist the reader can find fascinating, but also abhor. There cannot be one without the other lest the narrative lose its driving force.

And so it is with that ancient epic known as the Bible, particularly The Book of Revelation. Only in the former, the protagonist is God and the antagonist is Satan, and in the latter the protagonist is Jesus and the necessary antagonist is the one called the Beast, the dreaded Antichrist, the obligatory villain in the would-be greatest saga of them all.

Although the Antichrist has been an object of curiosity for the last 2000 years without actually appearing on the world scene, there is no shortage of would-be soothsayers these days who are convinced that the age of the Antichrist is imminent – if not already here.

In her 1969 autobiography, *My Life and Prophecies*, self-proclaimed psychic Jeane Dixon claimed to have envisioned the birth of the Antichrist on February 5, 1962. Dixon identified him as a direct descendant of Queen Nefertiti and the pharaoh Ikhnaton and indicated that he was born in the Middle East. She went on to predict that we would begin to "feel his presence" in the 1980s and that he would reach the pinnacle of his power in the ominous year of 1999.

Not only did Dixon's Antichrist fail to turn up in the 1980's, the 1990's and the decade that followed, but if alive today he would be at least 50 years old – well past his prime as the young, charismatic polar opposite of Jesus of Nazareth.

But in fairness to Ms. Dixon, she wasn't the only "prophet" to get it wrong. Everyone from Nostradamus to Reverend Jack Van Impe has been warning generation after generation that the big bad Beast would soon be coming to your neighborhood. So far, however, he's a no-show or, so the excuse goes, exists somewhere but is simply waiting for the right time to make his grand appearance.

The concept of an Antichrist, of course, comes from Chapter 13 of the Book of Revelation – also called The Apocalypse of Saint John the Apostle. It was written by John while he was held prisoner on the Greek island of Patmos and was intended for the seven Christian churches of Asia Minor to boost their morale during a brutal Roman persecution. The pertinent excerpt is as follows:

"And I saw a beast coming up out of the sea, having seven heads and ten horns, and upon its horns ten diadems, and upon its heads blasphemous names. And the beast that I saw was like a leopard, and its feet were like the feet of a bear, and its mouth like the mouth of a lion. And the dragon gave it his own might and great authority. And one of its heads was smitten, as it were, unto death; but its deadly wound was healed. And all the earth followed the beast in wonder. And they worshipped the dragon because he gave authority to the beast, and they worshipped the beast, saying, 'Who is like to the beast, and who will be able to fight with it?' (13: 1-4)

" … And it will cause all, the small and the great, and the rich and

the poor, and the free and the bond, to have a mark on their right hand or on their foreheads, and it will bring it about that no one may be able to buy or sell, except him who has the mark, either the name of the beast or the number of its name. Here is wisdom. He who has understanding, let him calculate the number of the beast, for it is the number of a man; and its number is six hundred and sixty-six."

According to Biblical scholars, including the Reverend John P. O'Connell, the most probable interpretation of the Beast's identity is that it represents the name Caesar Neron (Nero), which in Hebrew characters makes up the number of 666. It was, after all, during Nero's reign as Emperor of Rome that many Christians were brutally persecuted.

But such an interpretation has not satisfied those who expected more of the Apocalypse than the mere slaughter of Christian martyrs, thus the myth of an Antichrist has been perpetuated for many generations, making him the Keyser Söze – the ultimate bogeyman – of human history.

Over the centuries, there have been many suitable candidates for the title of Antichrist from Charlemagne to Genghis Khan to Napoleon Bonaparte to Josef Stalin. Some thought Adolf Hitler fit the bill – a genocidal dictator with a formidable army and global ambitions who could cast a spell over an entire nation with his passionate oratory and precipitate a world war. He even had a suitable mark of the beast – the crooked cross of the swastika – and had survived numerous assassination attempts. With his blitzkrieg of Poland and his merciless assault on the British Isles, some even wondered, *"Who is like to the beast, and who will be able to fight with it?"*

But as powerful and destructive as these figures were, none of them lived up to the expectations of the Antichrist described in Revelation, leaving the purveyors of Doomsday propaganda with no choice but to speculate that this supreme dictator was yet to flourish in an age of mass media, nuclear supremacy and religious conflict.

Subsequently, in these days of evangelical fervor and convoluted conjecture, the speculation has bordered on the ludicrous.

For example, every American president since Jimmy Carter has been an unlikely suspect. Yep, the peanut farmer from Georgia raised a few eyebrows when he brokered The Camp David Accords between Egypt's President Anwar Sadat and Israel's Prime Minister Menachem Begin in 1979. Was this the peace treaty that would commence a seven-year countdown to Armageddon in 1986?

Then it was Ronald Reagan's turn at bat. The Gipper, aka the Great Communicator, was thought by some to be the Beast by virtue of the fact that he had six letters in each of his names – Ronald Wilson Reagan (666 – get it?). Also, the winning numbers in both the Maryland and New Jersey lottery the day Reagan was first elected President were 6-6-6 – and the same numbers came up in the Maryland lottery the Saturday after his 1984 reelection (what more proof does one need?). The fact that Reagan was subsequently shot and recovered from his potentially mortal wound only added fuel to the speculation.

When Reagan's term ended – new prime suspects were needed. George H.W. Bush, Bill Clinton and George W. Bush – all were scrutinized as spawns of the devil in elaborate New World Order conspiracy theories.

Like Carter, Clinton acted as the go-between in an Israeli peace agreement in 1993 – this time between Prime Minister Shimon Peres and Palestinian leader Yasser Arafat. Also, his full name transliterated in Hebrew by the genatria equaled – you guessed it – 666.

Online conspiracy theorists also had a field day with Clinton's successor, George W. Bush. Through their paranoid prism, Bush 43 and his cabal of advisors were the real masterminds behind the September 11 attacks, using it as a pretext to spread war in the Middle East and impose new laws – like the Patriot Act – that limited personal freedom. But alas, the wars in Iraq and Afghanistan did not expand to other nations and Dubya's lack of interest in forcing a peace treaty between Israel and the Palestinians also threw a wet blanket on that theory.

And now, Barack Hussein Obama (18 letters = 6+6+6 – get it?) is the latest person of interest. There is even a Web site devoted to this notion based on circumstantial evidence. Coming out of relative obscurity to capture the Democratic nomination and win the presidency in 2008, Obama was a compelling suspect. It also didn't help that he was youthful, well-spoken and prone to send a tingle up Chris Matthews' leg. Now all he needs to do is broker a Middle East peace treaty, declare himself God and survive an otherwise mortal head wound to meet the requirements of the Armageddon in our lifetime crowd.

However, most end times enthusiasts dismiss the notion that the Antichrist will be an American. Many see him (not *her* oddly enough) as either a Middle Easterner or a member of the European Union – or even the Royal Family. Yes, there are those who are convinced that Bonnie Prince Charlie, who has yet to be elevated to the British throne, is the Beast.

The idea of the Prince of Wales, arguably one of the least magnetic figures of our day, being the Antichrist is based on several flimsy factors: He is believed to be descended from King David, Jesus and Mohammed. He spearheads an effort for enforceable environmentalism worldwide. He initiated the Global Security Programme and has partnered with the United Nations and the World Bank. He was born in 1948, the year of the establishment of the State of Israel. The phrase "Prince Charles of Wales" equals 666 when the number is transmuted from Hebrew/Greek numbering into the English alphabet.

Juan Carlos I, the King of Spain, has been subject to similar scrutiny on the basis of his having been born in Rome and being the leader of the 11th nation to join the revived Roman Empire (otherwise known to apocalyptic theorists as the European Union), fitting the prophecy of the "prince who will come" in Daniel 7: 23-25. He also hosted the 1991 Madrid Conference between Israel, Syria, Jordan and Lebanon, and we all know that the road to hell is paved with good intentions.

Meanwhile, a number of psychics point to hard-line Russian Prime Minister Vladimir Putin as the once and future Antichrist, no doubt because of his solid power base, stern disposition and unyielding diplomatic skills. But then the Antichrist is supposed to rise from the "sea" – not the KGB – and at this stage of the game, it's hard to conceive of a scenario in which the humorless and aging Putin will leave the world spellbound and compliant to his will.

Another target of suspicion – at least among some political conservatives – is billionaire George Soros by virtue of his political activism and influence on the world's currency markets. After all, it was he who made billions of dollars during the 1992 UK currency crisis when he correctly anticipated the devaluation of the pound sterling. Dubbed "The Man Who Broke The Bank of England," the Hungarian-born Soros may indeed be the political puppet master some claim he is. However, it is hard to consider an octogenarian philanthropist with no military or religious clout as a viable Antichrist.

Many evangelicals are convinced that the Beast – or his prophesized false prophet – will come from the Vatican. Pope John Paul II's recovery from a near fatal assassination attempt in 1981 raised some suspicion until the Pontiff's staunch support of traditional dogma and anti-communism put those fears to rest. This notion of a pontiff as an evil messianic figure stems from the Reformation and years of distrust and prejudice between Catholics and Protestants.

The only Asian candidate who seemed to be an Antichrist in sheep's clothing in the late 1970's and 1980's was the Reverend Sun Myung Moon. As founder of the Unification Church, Moon actually declared himself "the world's new Messiah" and "the Lord of the Second Advent." He then proceeded to perform mass weddings and established the global media conglomerate News World Communications, which includes *The Washington Times* and other newspapers, mixing religion and politics. Now in his 90's, the Korean-born Reverend Moon seems less of a covert satanic threat and more of a harmless, run-of-the-mill capitalist.

According to Nostradamus' more creative interpreters, the 16th century seer assigned the name Mabus to the last of three Antichrists. For a time, some thought this was an anagram for Saddam – as in Saddam Hussein, who seemed a logical choice until he ended up dangling from a hangman's noose and wasn't revived.

Meanwhile, Iranian President Mahmoud Ahmadinejad has the Hitler vibe going for him – what with his provocative threats against Israel and the United States plus his ongoing defiance of international sanctions aimed at discouraging the construction of Iranian nuclear facilities, but so far his bark is worse than his bite and there is little chance he can rally support among moderate Muslims in a future jihad against the West. A better candidate is the youthful Muqtada, al-Sadr, the stern-faced Iraqi Shi'a cleric and ayatollah in training, who some are touting as the Twelfth Iman.

Interestingly, Nostradamus' Quatrain 5 from Century VI refers to someone or something called Samarobin who will "live without law, exempt from politics" and cause "a very great famine through pestilence." Surprisingly, no one has suggested that Samarobin is an anagram for the late Osama Bin (Laden). Others pegged the Al-Qaeda leader and architect of the September 11th attacks as the "King of Terror" of Century X, Quatrain 72, but that was as far as it went. Obviously, it was difficult for Bin Laden to claim the crown of Antichrist when he was a fugitive from justice holed up in a cave and a Pakistani compound.

And then there are those who have their suspicions about King Abdullah of Jordan. For one thing, they note, he was born on January 30, 1962 – within a week of psychic Jeane Dixon's predicted "Child of the East." A direct descendant of the prophet Mohammed, he was educated in the United States and Oxford and is seen by many modern Muslims as the al-Mahdi (the savior to Islam), making him the ideal unifier of Western and Middle Eastern cultures. And according to Isaiah 10:12 and 14:25, the Antichrist will come from Assyria, part of what is now the Hashemite Kingdom of Jordan. It is nonetheless difficult to imagine a scenario in which the leader of a relatively small Islamic nation would be handed the reins of power over a vast, one-world government.

Although the Antichrist has yet to materialize, he has already cultivated a following among millions of readers and moviegoers. Fiction and non-fiction books devoted to the subject are plentiful, as are dramatizations of his future exploits.

On the screen, the Antichrist has been most notably portrayed by New Zealander Sam Neill (in *The Omen 3 – The Final Conflict*) and British actor Michael York (in *The Omega Code*) – politically correct choices unlikely to offend Muslims, Jews or Eurasians. Whereas Neill's Damien Thorn was a dark, deceitfully dashing and dangerous devil, York's Alexander Stone was a less charismatic, dryly diplomatic New World Order type who seemed better suited for a position in the House of Lords than as the master of all he surveys.

Author Stephen King had his own take on the End Times and its leading man in his novel *The Stand*. The action takes place in a post-apocalyptic America where a band of worthy survivors of a super virus have a date with destiny against sinister forces led by a mysterious dude named Randall Flagg – King's implied Antichrist. The final confrontation between good and evil (Armageddon) occurs in – of all places – Las Vegas, Nevada (Sin City, indeed), with the mighty hand of God wielding a nuclear missile to cast Satan into a lake of fire (figuratively and literally speaking). While *The Stand* is more of an homage to H.R. Tolkien's *The Lord of the Rings* than an interpretation of the Book of Revelation, the influence of the latter is undeniable.

Over the last half century or so there has been so much anticipation surrounding the arrival of the Antichrist and so much written and debated about his characteristics and the circumstances of his ascent that he would probably be recognizable even before he revealed his true identity. There is already intense scrutiny of every potential leader on the world scene – it is doubtful a false messiah could, to paraphrase Lincoln, fool all of the people all of the time.

Be that as it may, the mere possibility of such an all-powerful demagogue continues to fill pews and line the coffers of doomsday profiteers. Heroes are a dime a dozen, but villains are worth their weight in gold. In fact …

Memo to Milton Bradley: Guess Who's The Antichrist would make a great parlor game. Talk about an icebreaker.

CHAPTER 9

Apocalypse *When?*

*"Nah, nah, you don't believe we're on the eve of destruction." –
P.F. Sloan*

AT THE HEIGHT of the Cold War, President John F. Kennedy said the
world was living with a nuclear sword of Damocles hanging over
its head. That may still be true, but in more recent decades the perceived threats of extinction seem to have multiplied – some of them
valid, but most of them irrational. Nevertheless, there is no scarcity of
uneducated guesses on when the world will end – and a long list of
failed predictions.

Although Jesus himself said that no one "but the Father" knows
exactly when the world will end, that hasn't stopped some Christians
and Bible scholars from marking their calendars with a specific or
approximate expiration date. Not surprisingly, every time they think
they've figured out when and how the curtain will fall, the pious pundits are always wrong.

For most of our modern doomsday devotees the Last Judgment
is always just around the corner. Others have treated it like a moving target. For years the Jehovah's Witnesses predicted the end of
the world by 1975. Naturally, they insisted that only their followers
would achieve eternal salvation as a reward, the same prize offered
by virtually every religion. After that fateful year came and went, the

Jehovah's Witnesses continued to point to impending doom, although they ceased to mention a specific date.

Similarly, Indian Hindus headed for the hills in February of 1962 when the planets of our solar system were in alignment – a sure sign, they believed, that the world was ending. Although the Cuban Missile Crisis later that year provided a glimmer of affirmation for the fatalists that mankind's extinction was a distinct possibility, the crisis passed and it was back to Cold War politics as usual for another two decades.

By far the most prolific – and one of the most prosperous – exponents of Doomsday fear-mongering has been Hal Lindsey, co-author of *The Late Great Planet Earth* (along with Carole C. Carlson). Like Jeane Dixon, his religious and political soul mate, Lindsey predicted the coming of the Antichrist in the 1980's. Not only that – he and Carlson also threw in the Rapture, the tribulation and the Second Coming of Christ, all of which he led readers to believe would occur before the end of the 20th century.

Published in 1970, *The Late Great Planet Earth* based its postulation on the interpretation of a quote in the Gospel According to Matthew (24: 32-34) that allegedly indicated that Jesus would return within "one generation" of the establishment of the state of Israel and the rebuilding of the Jewish Temple. One generation in the Bible, according to Lindsey, was approximately 40 years. So, by that measurement, the Apocalypse was supposed to occur by 1988.

Using Biblical prophecy from both the Old and New Testaments, Lindsey's book conjured a vision of a not-so-distant future exploding with war, famine, earthquakes and totalitarianism preceding the Second Coming. A graduate of Dallas Theological Seminary and a former staff member of Campus Crusade for Christ, Lindsey offered readers one hope of survival from the horrors predicted in his book – the acceptance of Christ as their savior.

In 1980, Lindsey published a follow-up book entitled *The 1980s: Countdown to Armageddon* in which he reiterated his claim that the End Times were imminent. In both books, Lindsey maintained – like others before him – that the Antichrist would rise from a ten-member or ten-nation European confederacy (i.e. the European Union), which would represent a revival of the Roman Empire. During this time of tribulation, the Russians would invade Israel and famines, wars and earthquakes would all serve as signs that the end of the world was upon us.

The first Christian book of prophecy to be released by a secular publishing house, *The Late Great Planet Earth* was the biggest nonfiction bestseller of the decade, selling more than 8 million copies by 1978 and another 20 million copies by 1990. An amazing feat – considering that none of what is predicted in the book has come to pass.

When Lindsey's 1988 deadline for Armageddon came and went, he revised his forecast. Israel, he maintained, did not acquire land until the six-day war of 1967, therefore the end of the world would not come until 40 years after 1967 – in 2007 with the Rapture occurring in 2000. When nothing happened between 2000 and 2007, Lindsey deferred the fateful date again – now claiming that a generation was actually 60-80 years, not 40, thus placing the Rapture in 2040 and the Last Judgment in 2047. Now that's what you call creative accounting.

When Lindsey isn't dubiously deciphering the Book of Revelation, he serves as a religious, right-wing commentator on The Hal Lindsey Report website and Trinity Broadcasting Network television program of the same name, attributing many of the apocalyptic forces brewing in the world to the left-wing agenda of liberals in the U.S. government. In other words, he has an ideological and political axe to grind. And even though Lindsey repeatedly has been wrong when it comes to predicting the end of the world, he just can't or won't stop himself – at least not as long as the royalty checks keep coming in.

One of the most irrational and comical doomsday journals appeared in the early 1980's under the name of *The Last Trumpet*. Published by Willie and David Hauser of Amityville, Long Island, the tabloid offered its readers "Tomorrow's News Today" with screaming apocalyptic headlines such as "RUSSIA INVADES MIDEAST," "WORLD FACES ECONOMIC COLLAPSE," "MESSIAH RETURNS AS ALL NATIONS GATHER TO DESTROY ISRAEL," as well as unintentionally amusing future news like "MILLIONS MISSING – WHERE ARE THEY?" and this laughably hysterical description of anarchy afoot on the West Coast: "*Moral decay in California has become epidemic … Drug and alcohol use is out of control as the overdose rate has tripled in the last six months … Many desperate people have turned to the occult and rival gangs of witches are murdering each other by the hundreds … Sexual perversion has erupted as homosexual mobs roam the streets committing atrocities against women and children … Law enforcement agencies appear to be helpless as we approach total chaos …* (And here's the kicker) *The governor is now considering putting the state under martial law.*"

And all this for just 25 cents a copy!

The Last Trumpet was obviously nothing more than an imitator of the Hal Lindsey blueprint for Armageddon with the typical religious payoff ("BIBLE SEARCH PROVES WORLD WAS WARNED") followed by two full pages of scripture and evangelical interpretation. The end result looked more like parody (perhaps something concocted by *The Onion*) than prophecy.

Nearly 30 years after the publication of *The Last Trumpet*, we're all still waiting for the Rapture, the gangs of Deatheaters and the attack of the gay zombies. Somewhere Criswell Predicts is laughing his ass off.

In 1982, all of the planets in our solar system (including Pluto, which has since been demoted to the rank of dwarf planet) aligned on the same side of the sun, an event that only happens once every 179 years. Predictably, this raised concerns about the fate of the Earth. And this time, even the scientific community and establishment media got in on the act. An article in the September 16, 1974 issue of *Newsweek* warned, "Scientists are forecasting that soon our solar system will experience some unique and sobering events." The magazine featured John Gribbin, science editor of *Nature*, and Stephen Plagemann of NASA's Goddard Space Center in Maryland, co-authors of the book, *The Jupiter Effect*, floating the idea that just as the moon's gravitational force affects ocean tides, other planets

– especially Jupiter – have the same effect on each other. Gribbin and Plagemann maintained that when all the planets align, they exert a united gravitational pull on the Earth with eight "probable effects":

1. Disturbed magnetic activity in the sun, resulting in huge firestorms;
2. A change in the Earth's ionosphere;
3. Disruption of radio and television communications;
4. Weird lighting effects from aurora borealis;
5. Vast changes in wind patterns;
6. A change in rainfall and temperature patterns;
7. A possible change in the Earth's rotation; and
8. A significant increase in seismic activity. It was even suggested that the event could trigger a long overdue earthquake (the Big One) for California.

The planets lined up on March 10, 1982, the world held its breath, and … nothing happened before, during or after that date. In an attempt to wipe the egg off their faces, Messrs. Gribbin and Plagemann then claimed that the Jupiter effect had actually occurred in 1980 – when the planets weren't aligned – and caused the Mount St. Helen volcanic eruption. Okay …

In 1983, one Bhangwan Shree Rajneesh, a guru of the Rajneesh movement joined the Chicken Little Club by declaring that the earth was entering a 15-year period – leading up to the dreaded year 1999 – of catastrophic destruction. On the menu were massive floods, earthquakes, volcanoes and a nuclear war – all of which would wipe out major cities including Tokyo, New York, San Francisco, Los Angeles and Bombay. Frisco took a bit of a hit in 1989, as did part of L.A. in 1994, but both recovered quite nicely. Otherwise, zilch.

Armageddon was slated for 1986, according to Moses David of a faith group called The Children of God. In this scenario, both Israel and the United States would fall to the Soviet Union, which would then establish a worldwide dictatorship that would be defeated in

1993 with the Second Coming of Christ. Instead, the Soviet Union collapsed, the U.S. and Israel are still in business, and the faithful are still waiting for you know who.

Something called the Harmonic Convergence was hyped by New Age futurists in 1987. Based on Hopi mythology, it involved the second coming of the serpent god of peace around August 16-17 – and had nothing to do with harmonicas. Apparently, it also had nothing to do with harmony, either, as world peace continued to be an elusive goal well into the 21st century.

In 1988, a timely book called *88 Reasons Why the Rapture Is In 1988* created a bit of a stir in religious circles. Many of the "Beam Me Up, Scotty" bumper sticker crowd bought the book, took it to heart and prepared for an abrupt ascent into heaven. When the deadline of September 11-13 passed and the faithful were still grounded, the book's author Edgar Whisenaunt wrote another book entitled *89 Reasons Why the Rapture Is In 1989*, obviously testing the old adage, "If at first you don't succeed …" To no one's surprise – except perhaps Mr. Whisenaunt – the second book wasn't nearly as successful as the first.

Then, with the start of the Gulf War in 1991, a number of evangelicals gleefully proclaimed that Armageddon had finally arrived. In this scenario, Saddam was Nostradamus' Mabus or the Book of Revelation's Antichrist, and his invasion of Kuwait coupled with his missile attack on Israel would trigger World War III. Instead, of course, Coalition forces drove the Iraqi army all the way back to Baghdad in less than 30 days and there was no subsequent showdown in the Valley of Meggido. So it was back to the drawing board for the Doomsday scenarists.

The next major deadline for Doomsday was 1999. Not only was there the famous Nostradamus prediction about "the King of Terror" coming from the sky in the seventh month of that year, but Jeane Dixon had also predicted that a cross would appear in the heavens signaling the return of the Messiah. 1999 came and went and there were no sightings of floating crosses in the firmament – not even one created by a zealous skywriter. Neither did Nostradamus' prediction come true. In fact, considering the amount of anticipation that had been building, 1999 was a relatively uneventful year.

So it was on to 2000 and 2001, when tabloids like *The Globe* and *The National Enquirer* frequently ran imminent Doomsday prophecy stories that didn't pan out. The only events that added fuel to their provocative speculation were the burst of the dot.com bubble and, of course, the September 11th attacks. The latter, coupled with a subsequent anthrax scare, was hyped as the official start of the road to Armageddon. A decade later, however, the never-ending death watch continues.

In 2008 Ronald Weiland, pastor of the Worldwide Church of God and author of *The Prophesied End-Time* and *2008 – God's Final Witness*, declared himself one of the two witnesses of Revelation. He also predicted that 2008 would mark the beginning of a three-and-a-half-year countdown to the end of mankind's self-rule. According to Weiland, the First Trumpet of the Seventh Seal of the Book of Revelation would sound on December 14, 2008, signaling the collapse of the U.S. economy. Three more trumpets would follow to mark the complete collapse of the United States, followed by a final trumpet triggering World War III.

While the economic prediction was too close for comfort, the other trumpets so far have sounded more like kazoos. In his second book, Weiland claimed that six seals have already been opened and the world is ignoring them. He also predicted that by January 2009, the United States would "be down the tubes." He then suggested that nuclear weapons will be detonated in major American cities any day now and that Jesus Christ would return by the fall of 2011. "If it doesn't come to pass … then I'm nothing but a false prophet," wrote Weiland. Now that's something we can all believe.

Finally, in 2011, Christian radio broadcaster Harold Camping generated a lot of press by predicting the Rapture would occur on May 21 followed by five months of tribulation on Earth culminating in the end of the world on October 21. Camping, the president of

California-based Family Radio applied numerology to his interpretation of Bible passages to determine Judgment Day – the same way he previously predicted it on May 21, 1988, and September 7, 1994. Convinced that the third time would be the charm, Camping and his followers were quite dismayed when the first deadline came and went. Shortly thereafter, the never-say-survive believer checked his numbers again and explained that he had miscalculated. A "spiritual" judgment had indeed occurred on May 21 and the real fireworks (Rapture, destruction, Final Judgment) would occur on October 21.

On June 9, 2011, the 89-year old Camping reportedly suffered a stroke and was hospitalized, and was later moved to a nursing home. Some Christian organizations opposed to Camping's pronouncements speculated that it was a punishment from God for his "heresies." *(Mind you, this was in 2011.)* His radio show, *Open Forum*, was summarily replaced with new programming. Meanwhile, October 21 passed without incident. So did Halloween.

And so, now that all these dates with destiny have failed to materialize, the undaunted forces of doom and gloom are pinning all their hopes of vindication on one more day of reckoning – December 21, 2012.

That, of course, is when the Mayan calendar comes to an abrupt end, signifying – what else? – the end of the world. Whether this will prove to be another non-event and thus their Waterloo or yet another "beginning of the beginning of the end" remains to be seen. But as one little boy discovered in a famous tale, you can only cry wolf so many times before people turn a deaf ear to your rantings.

But as long as there are converts and customers for this curious obsession, expect the howling to continue.

CHAPTER **10**

Let Us Prey

"All religions are founded on the fear of the many and the cleverness of a few." -- Stendhal

AS PREVIOUSLY NOTED, organized religion and end times profiteering seem to go hand in hand. A century has not gone by without the threat of The Last Judgment being held over mankind's head by certain religious institutions or by individual clerics whose purposes were not entirely selfless. But if the hierarchy of the major sects tends to steer away from the blatant exploitation of apocalyptic fears, the American evangelical movement of the latter 20th century has demonstrated no such reticence.

That's because evangelicals have the most to gain from Day of Reckoning mania – and the most to lose if their dire predictions do not come true. Many have gone out on a limb in their belief that these truly are the end of days – or at least the beginning of the end – that they'll have a lot of explaining to do if history doesn't play out the way they have predicted.

Whereas tent-posted, revival meeting preachers used to evoke fire and brimstone as the spur to indoctrinate their congregations – most Bible-thumpers today not only warn of the wrath of the Almighty, but also of the extortionist demands of the future Antichrist. Heaven help you if you don't get caught up in the Rapture. You'll be left behind to face the Great Tribulation and the awful choice of either becoming a martyr or accepting the mark of the Beast and the eternal damnation that goes with it.

The loss of Paradise has always been a ploy used by zealous clergymen. When science – or just plain common sense – challenged their beliefs, they resorted to psychological fear tactics to sustain the notion that religion is humanity's only refuge from destruction.

Now that mankind is capable of destroying itself with nuclear weapons, born-again zealots have found a more convincing means of driving home their ultimatum. They maintain that without obedience and unquestioning devotion to religious precepts, mankind becomes sinful and the punishment for sinfulness is plague, pestilence and perdition.

Reverend Pat Robertson, for example, insisted that AIDS was God's punishment against homosexuals and promiscuous hetero-sexuals – apparently considering monogamous adults and innocent children who contracted HIV through blood transfusion as merely collateral damage.

Robertson also implied that Hurricane Katrina took deadly aim on New Orleans because it was a sinful city, which doesn't exactly explain why his home base of Virginia Beach is often in the path of similar cyclones.

Even the more reputable of evangelists have used the apocalyptic approach to their advantage. The Reverend Billy Graham, who taught the Christian principles of humility and material poverty while golfing with presidents and managing to place on various "best-dressed" lists, dealt with the question of world upheaval and destruction in his bestselling volume, *The Road to Armageddon*. Again, the solution for an endangered world of varying cultures, creeds and economic conditions, according to Graham, was total submission to the Christian philosophy. Predictably, the book did nothing to enhance the human condition, but its profits enriched Graham's foundation and helped sustain his notoriety.

Evangelical pastors have even been known to play the Doomsday card to gain a competitive edge against other religions. Herbert W. Armstrong, the pastor general of the Worldwide Church of God until his death at the age of 93 in 1986, editor-in-chief of the *Plain Truth* magazine, television commentator on *It Is Written*, and author of several books including *The United States and Britain in Prophecy* had his own conspiracy theory about the Apocalypse.

As a globe-trotting harbinger of "kingdom come," Armstrong quoted scripture with every other sentence in an inexhaustible effort to alert and convert the masses before the great tribulation he envisioned.

What distinguished Armstrong from the pack of paranoid preachers was his rather controversial conclusion that it will be the Vatican that paves the way for mankind's seduction by Satan and that Rome may even become the seat of the Antichrist, a fear also expressed by the Our Lady of Fatima Crusade, an apocalypse-conscious faction of the Catholic Church.

The aforementioned Hal Lindsey, co-author of *The Late Great Planet Earth*, has also been guilty of the "my religion is better than your religion" tactic. Using Biblical prophecy from both the Old and New Testaments, Lindsey's book conjured a vision of a not-so-distant future exploding with war, famine, earthquakes and totalitarianism preceding the Second Coming of Jesus Christ.

A graduate of Dallas Theological Seminary and a former staff member of Campus Crusade for Christ, Lindsey offered readers one hope of survival from the horrors predicted in his book – the acceptance of Christ as their savior.

The proliferation of religious propaganda throughout *The Late Great Planet Earth* was so excessive that it read like a recruitment manual rather than a prophetic warning. The reader was constantly reminded that all forces in the world either positive or negative are governed by God or Satan.

The height of Lindsey's born-again conceit was reached when he predicted that Jews will finally accept Christ as their messiah just prior to the Last Judgment.

And then there's Dr. Jack Van Impe, the venerable host of television's *Jack Van Impe Presents,* a weekly Evangelical end-time prophecy show that has been on the air since the mid-1980's. On each episode, Van Impe copiously interprets scripture and obsessively proselytizes while his more subdued but equally fervent wife and co-host Rexella provides current news headlines that appear to validate Van Impe's rants. Once that's done, the pair turns the mike over to deep-voiced pitchman Chuck Ohman, who chimes in with a commercial for the Jack Van Impe Ministries' latest instructional end-time video.

Much like Hal Lindsey and Herbert Armstrong, Van Impe is convinced that the European Union is the revived Roman Empire from which the Antichrist will rise, hastening Armageddon and all the fun times that will go with it.

In 2001, Van Impe published *On The Edge of Eternity* wherein he predicted that the year would *"usher in international chaos such as we've never seen in our history."* This, he predicted, would be the beginning of an era in which the world would be plagued by *"drought, war, malaria, and hunger afflicting entire populations throughout the* [African] *continent."* He also forecast that Islam would become much larger than Christianity, a one-world church would emerge and it would be *"controlled by demonic hosts."*

The bit about Africa was true – and had been the case for many years in the 20th century – but the rest didn't pan out as Dr. Van Impe had envisioned. But then again, this is the man who's been warning that the Rapture, Antichrist Armageddon, and the Second Coming were just around the corner for some 25 odd years. And I do mean odd.

For the record, nowhere in the Bible does it say that there will be a seven-year tribulation. This was a myth that evolved from several key sources, including a Jesuit priest named Ribera who, in 1591, invented a futurist view of Biblical prophecy as a means of preventing reformers from teaching that the Catholic Church was the "whore of Babylon" envisioned on Revelation 17:3-6.

Ribera maintained that the prophecies in the Book of Revelation would not be fulfilled until the end of the Christian era. He also advanced the notion of a revived Babylon, the rebuilding of the temple in Jerusalem and the arrival of an end-time Antichrist.

In 1731, a Spanish Catholic priest living in Chile named Manuel de Lacunza y Diaz moved to Imola, Italy where he claimed to be a converted Jew named Rabbi Juan Jushafat Ben-Ezra and wrote a book entitled *The Coming of Messiah in Glory and Majesty*. De Lacunza introduced the theory – derived from the Book of Daniel – that the faithful would be taken to heaven 45 days before the second coming of Christ. During that 45-day period, God would unleash his great misery on those unworthy inhabitants of Earth left behind. Thus was born the theory of a pre-tribulation rapture.

Then, in the 19th century, a wee Scottish girl named Margaret McDonald claimed to have had a vision in which the church was secretly raptured. Beguiled, an evangelist by the name of Robert Norton felt compelled to preach this revelation throughout England. Apparently it caught on because today it is an erroneous cornerstone of the whole evangelical belief system.

Lest one think that the end times are the exclusive domain of Christian evangelicals, figureheads of other religions have also tried their hand at putting modern conflicts into an apocalyptic context. For example, at the start of the Gulf War in 1991, Nation of Islam Leader Louis Farrakhan predicted it would be "the War of Armageddon … the final war."

Outright charlatans have thrived as well on the grim realities of the atomic era. One of Reverend Jim Jones' most persuasive excuses why the People's Temple members had to relocate to the jungles of Guyana in the 1970's was the alleged inevitability of Armageddon. He convinced his disciples that a third world war was imminent and only those who followed him to his remote tropical paradise would survive the holocaust. They obeyed and ironically doomed themselves to a self-induced holocaust by drinking cyanide-laced Kool-Aid.

Another member of the Apocalyptic Hall of Shame was David Koresh (aka Vernon Wayne Howell), leader of the Branch Davidian religious sect in Waco, Texas who in 1992 changed the name of his cult's commune from Mount Carmel to Ranch Apocalypse based on the belief that the battle of Armageddon would begin at the compound. Indeed, all hell broke loose when Koresh, accused of coercion, child abuse and statutory rape refused to surrender to federal agents in a raid by the U.S. Bureau of Alcohol, Tobacco, Firearms and Explosives that claimed the lives of four agents and six members of the sect.

According to the Branch Davidians, the world would end in 1995. But for Koresh and his followers – 54 adults and 21 children – the end came on April 10, 1993 when, after a 51-day stand-off with federal agents, the compound burned to the ground.

Newly appointed Attorney General Janet Reno and the Clinton administration took the heat for the tragedy, especially from "black helicopter" conspiracy theorists. But evidence presented in an official investigation – the Danforth Report – showed that the fire was deliberately set from within the compound and that numerous Branch Davidians – including Koresh – had been shot as part of a mass murder/suicide pact.

One would think that end-times religious figures would want to forestall the apocalypse as long as possible to keep those contributions and sales coming in. But a number of congregations are actually trying to *hasten* the event in the belief that the sooner it occurs, the sooner they'll be raptured to heaven.

In fact, mega-church pastors from around the United States convened in Inglewood, California in February of 2006 to plan for the fulfillment of the Great Commission, an instruction from the resurrected Jesus Christ to his apostles that they spread his teachings to all the nations of the world. Once that mission is accomplished, Christians believe, the path will be paved for the Second Coming

Of course, reaching more than 6 billion people will take something of a miracle – and lots and lots of donations. But the pastors are convinced it's doable through global communications, aircraft to transport missionaries, and the establishment of five million new churches by 2016.

At the same time, the evangelical Promise Keepers movement, co-founded by Bill McCartney and dedicated to "uniting men to become 'godly influences' in the world," has its own ambitious agenda called The Road to Jerusalem.

The project's goal, in the organization's words, is "mobilizing the body of Christ to partner with the Jewish believer for the salvation of Israel, thus the world." In layman's terms: Convert as many Jews to Christianity as possible before Jesus' returns and anyone who is not a born-again Christian goes to hell. Good luck with that, Bill.

With each passing year and unfulfilled end-times prophecy, you'd think the converted would wise up and un-covert themselves.

But true believers are a stubborn and patient breed, clinging to the belief that the Rapture will come sooner or later, and if it's later it'll be worth the wait. In fact, according to various surveys, an estimated 40% of Americans believe that the end times are already underway.

In the meantime, however, their spiritual guides, none of whom have taken a vow of poverty, are bringing home the bacon. According to Giving USA, religious organizations received $106.89 billion in donations in 2008 alone. That's almost twice as much as Apple or Microsoft makes in annual revenue.

It is the great irony of history that more people have been persecuted, tortured, enslaved and slaughtered in the name of organized religion than in any pagan holocaust. But what really adds insult to injury is when religious charlatans want your money as well as your blood. One can only hope *their* day of reckoning will come sooner, rather than later.

CHAPTER 11

No Profit Left Behind

"This is not a novel to be tossed aside lightly. It should be thrown with great force." – Dorothy Parker

IN THE PANTHEON of great ideas for a page-turning novel, one of the best – and certainly most influential – was Ira Levin's *Rosemary's Baby*. Published in 1967, *Rosemary's Baby* was the tale of a young woman who moves into a Gothic New York City apartment building (much like the Dakota) with her husband, a struggling actor, and soon discovers that her elderly neighbors are part of a coven with a vested interest in her unborn child – a child that is actually the son of Satan.

Rosemary's Baby was an instant bestseller, topping the *New York Times* fiction list and spawning an equally provocative and devilishly entertaining film directed by Roman Polanski and released in 1968. For better or worse, it also inspired other demonic thrillers including the highly successful *The Exorcist* and, particularly, *The Omen*, which more elaborately expanded on the mythology of the Antichrist, as well as a host of end-times millennial literature. But more about that in a moment.

First, allow me to share a related anecdote. When the film version of *The Omen* – also about the Son of Satan and future Antichrist – was released on June 25, 1976, I found the date more than a bit curious. It happened to be the 10th birthday of Adrian (aka Andrew), Ira Levin's

NO PROFIT LEFT BEHIND ❧

Antichrist in *Rosemary's Baby*. I wrote a letter to Mr. Levin pointing this out as if it had some cosmic significance, eluding to the fact that the number 666 upside down was 999 and that Adrian would be 33 years old (the same age as Jesus when he died) in 1999.

Mr. Levin was kind enough to reply, politely humoring my hare-brained "revelations." As the voice of reason, he dismissed the release date of *The Omen* as a mere coincidence, referred to his character as *Andrew* (the name his mother Rosemary gave him), and stated his doubt that anything apocalyptic would happen in 1999. And, of course, he was right.

Nevertheless, in 1997 Ira Levin saw fit to write a sequel to his most famous novel entitled *Son of Rosemary*, which took place in 1999 with a 33 year-old Adrian/Andrew now heading a worldwide chari-table organization with 12 assistants (disciples) and being courted by the Republican Party and the Religious Right to endorse a candidate for president. While critics of the sequel felt Levin should have left well enough alone and quit while he was ahead, it's awfully hard to resist the temptation to go back to the well. Guess you could say the devil made him do it.

On the other hand, it's easy to tell what possessed authors Tim LaHaye and Jerry B. Jenkins from turning their wildly popular novel *Left Behind: A Novel of the Earth's Last Days* into a continuing series. In fact, these end-times chronicles have become a cottage industry all their own. Although there have been a number of forerunners, including *The Omen* novelizations, the *Left Behind* series represents the most ambitious serialization of Christian apocalyptic fiction.

Among LaHaye and Jenkins' predominantly evangelical audi-ence, the big question, "Which came first, the chicken or the egg?" has been replaced with "Which comes first, the rapture or the trib-ulation?" For the *Left Behind* series, La Haye and Jenkins elect the pre-tribulation, premillenial, Christian eschatological viewpoint – in plain English, the Rapture comes first.

The plot in a nutshell: It's the End Times, true believers are rap-tured and the world they leave behind is thrown into chaos. Earthly survivors of the event are at a loss to explain where their missing families and friends have gone. Along comes a knight in shining armor in the person of Nicolae Carpathia, a Romanian politician who becomes Secretary-General of the United Nations, promising to restore peace and order. What few realize, however, is that Carpathia is actually the Antichrist. Several characters who know the truth become born-again Christians and create the Tribulation Force, a group dedicated to saving as many souls as possible and preparing them for a seven-year period of hell on earth.

You would think such a story – inspired of course by the prophecies of the Book of Revelation, Isaiah and Ezekiel as interpreted by dispensationalists – could be told in one epic novel. But that would be underestimating its profit potential.

Like the tales of Scheherazade, the *Left Behind* saga goes on and on and on. There have been no less than 16 novels in the *Left Behind* series – all of them bestsellers. In fact, if you think the Harry Potter books were a phenomenon, consider this – the first four *Left Behind* books held the top four positions on the *New York Times'* Bestsellers' list simultaneously in 1998 and the tenth book debuted at number one in 2002. Seven of the books have reached the number one spot on the *Times*, *USA Today* and *Publishers Weekly* lists. All told, the Left Behind series has sold an estimated 70 million copies worldwide (oddly enough, the approximate number of Americans who identify themselves as evangelicals).

In chronological order, the books include:

Left Behind: A Novel of the Earth's Last Days
Tribulation Force: The Continuing Drama of Those Left Behind
Nicolae: The Rise of Antichrist
Soul Harvest: The World Takes Sides
Apollyon: The Destroyer Is Unleashed
Assassins: Assignment: Jerusalem, Target: Antichrist
The Indwelling: The Beast Takes Possession
The Mark: The Beast Rules the World

Desecration: Antichrist Takes the Throne
The Remnant: On the Brink of Armageddon
Armageddon: The Cosmic Battle of the Ages
Glorious Appearing: The End of Days
The Rising: Antichrist is Born: Before They Were Left Behind
The Regime: Evil Advances: Before They Were Left Behind #2
The Rapture: In the Twinkling of an Eye: Countdown to Earth's Last Days #3
Kingdom Come: The Final Victory

Not just an American obsession, the *Left Behind* series has been translated into many languages and proven popular in Asian countries such as China and Japanese, and in Latin America as well. Not so much, however, in Europe where dispensationalists are considered the lunatic fringe of American culture.

As if that weren't enough, the publishers and promoters behind the collection have spun off two other series, *Left Behind: Apocalypse* by Mel Odom and *Left Behind: End of State* by Neesa Hart, not to mention a *Left Behind: The Kids* series for teenagers with the same plot as the original series, but with adolescents as the main protagonists. No demographic left behind, eh? It is estimated that *The Kids* series, audio books and comic books alone are worth $100 million in annual revenue.

Oh, and let's not forget the *Left Behind* graphic novels, CDs, and movies. The series has thus far spawned three action-thriller films produced by Cloud Ten Pictures: *Left Behind: The Movie* (2000), *Left Behind II: Tribulation Force* (2002) and *Left Behind: World at War (2005)* starring real-life evangelist and former *Growing Pains* cast member Kirk Cameron.

In a marketing campaign as baffling as the Book of Revelation, the first film was released on video and DVD *first*, then booked into theatres where it performed poorly. The sequel went straight to video, debuted in the #2 spot on the Nielson's video scan report and reached the #1 sales ranking for two days on Amazon.com.

There has even been a trio of PC video games – *Left Behind: Eternal Forces*, *Left Behind: Tribulation Forces*, and *Left Behind 3: Rise of the Antichrist*. The first product raked in $2.2 million in sales in its first quarter. But all three games triggered protests from the Christian Alliance For Progress, American Atheists and the Anti-Defamation League for their excessive violence and alleged religious intolerance and a campaign urging Wal-Mart to stop selling them.

All that's missing, it seems, is a Left Behind theme park in Branson, Missouri or Orlando, Florida. Just imagine it – attractions could include the Rapture Rollercoaster, the Tribulation Force log flume, the Temple Mount boutique, Mark of the Beast interactive games for the kids, the Armageddon 3D Experience, the New Jerusalem Café, and a live musical show enactment of the Second Coming.

But for all the fanfare, it wasn't until the *Left Behind* series was the subject of a parody in an episode of *The Simpsons* called "Left Below" that it was clearly became a noteworthy part of our pop culture. In the episode, non-Christians, gays and folks who believe in science miss the Rapture and must live in a hellish world, which kind of puts the whole end-times craze in its proper comedic context.

Other critics of the Left Behind saga haven't been as good-natured. Among other complaints, the series has sparked charges of anti-Catholicism because a.) a minority of Catholics are raptured (that old "my religion is better than your religion" prejudice), b.) a fictional Pope John XXIV is raptured only because he accepted some of the views of Martin Luther (the titular father of Protestantism), and c.) the next Pope Peter II (thank you, St. Malachy) is named Pontifex Maximus of a new, all-embracing religion called Enigma Babylon One World Faith.

In a blistering special report entitled *False Profit: Money, Prejudice, and Bad Theology in Tim LaHaye's Left Behind Series*, author Jimmy Aikin underscores numerous examples of anti-Catholicism and maintains that there are two motives at odds in the *Left Behind* franchise:

"The first is a sincere desire to advance people's knowledge of God's prophetic words – what we may call a 'prophet motive.' The

second is the simple desire to make a buck – plain, old, ordinary profit motive ... The trouble is that his understanding of Bible prophecy is seriously defective. As a result, he spreads more error than knowledge. He leads people to needlessly obsess about and fear the future ... There is nothing wrong with financial success, but when the means by which one achieves it involves spreading error and fear, it is shameful. Worse, the profit motive seems to be the stronger of the two."

The series has also been criticized in some quarters as an affront to Judaism and liberal secularism. In order for Jews to reach heaven, the books imply, they must first accept Christ as their messiah.

Even a number of mainstream and premillenialist Christians have a problem with the *Left Behind* stories. Amillenial and postmillennial Christians have a different timeline for the Second Coming and preterist Christians don't even bother predicting future events via the Book of Revelation. Meanwhile, the choir LeHaye and Jenkins are preaching to – premillenialists – find it hard to reconcile the fact that some characters in the series are forced to receive the mark of the beast, yet still manage to be saved.

"The fictionalizing of Scripture is an egregious offense in and of itself," claimed a review by the Biblical Discernment Ministries, *"but the theology presented in the books is intolerable."*

The Commission on Theology and Church Relations of the Lutheran Church concurs: *"... the ideas expressed in the Left Behind series are in many ways contrary to the teaching of holy scripture. Though containing a fictional story line, the books promote a theology that is, in important respects, at odds with the biblical revelation."*

That, according to LeHaye, is nitpicking. In a 2000 interview for *Pentecostal Evangel* magazine, the co-author defended the series as *"the first fictional portrayal of events that are true to the literal interpretation of Bible prophecy. It was written for anyone who loves gripping fiction featuring believable characters, a dynamic plot that also weaves prophetic events into a fascinating story."*

Spoken like a true salesman. The only problem with that assessment is that *Left Behind* is not the first Rapture novel, nor is it the first

Rapture book with that title. It was preceded in January, 1996, by one written by Peter and Patti Lalonde. And accusations of plagiarism arose when similarities between *Left Behind* and the 1970 novel *666* by Salem Kirban came to light.

But as they say, success has many fathers, while failure is an orphan. And commercially speaking, the *Left Behind* series is anything but a failure. Striking while the iron is hot, LaHaye and Jenkins have tapped into millennial apocalyptic madness and given people what they want – a hot, succulent slice of pie in the sky.

Ten years from now, when the Temple Mount is still the site of an Islamic mosque, Israel and the Palestinians are still bickering, the European Union is still struggling to hold itself together, the Antichrist is nowhere to be seen, and no one has yet taken the express lane to paradise, hopefully the Left Behind series will assume its rightful place in literature – that is, left behind.

CHAPTER 12

Et Tu, Y2K?

"To err is human, but to really foul things up you need a computer." – Paul Ehrlich

REMEMBER THE COLLECTIVE apprehension that accompanied the turn of the latest millennium? The global fear factor manifested itself in a variety of perceived and actual threats.

For one thing, there was general paranoia over the year 1999 exacerbated by the predictions of multiple psychics. For years leading up to this dreaded date, disciples of Nostradamus were convinced that during the summer of that year, "The King of Terror" would come from the sky. Oddly enough, several terrorists – intent on blowing up Los Angeles International Airport – were caught several months later on New Year's Eve trying to smuggle explosives over the U.S.-Canadian border. Even the artist formerly and lately known as Prince musically proclaimed 1999 as the year of "party over, out of time."

But an even bigger concern had nothing to do with saboteurs, an alien invasion or the blowing of Gabriel's trumpet. It was something far more technologically insidious and – so we were warned – potentially dangerous to humanity's well-being. It was known by many names – the Year 2000 problem, the millennium bug, the Y2K bug, or just plain ol' Y2K.

Depending on which moniker was used, it sounded like a

contagious disease or a new form of germ warfare. And in the days leading up to January 1, 2000, it struck more horror into the hearts of computer geeks than anthrax.

And yet, to the layperson, Y2K was a menace hard to describe, let alone wrap your brain around its implications. It was a problem affecting both digital (i.e. computer-related) and non-digital documentation and data storage caused by the practice of abbreviating a four-digit year to two digits. In many of the existing computer programs at the time, the use of two digits to represent a year created errors when the year rolled over from x99 to x00.

The problem first came to light circa 1984 with the publication of the book, *Computers in Crisis* by Jerome and Marilyn Murray, reissued in 1996 with the title *The Year 2000 Computing Crisis*. Other books about the impending crisis promptly followed, though few of them were as scholarly or focused strictly on providing technical solutions.

As they were wont to do, many Fundamentalist Christians and evangelicals alarmists wrote books about the possible ramifications of the Millennium Bug that bordered on inciting panic. Some of the titles included Julian Gregori's *What Will Become of Us? Counting Down to Y2K* and *Y2K: The Day the World Shut Down* by Michael Hyatt and George E. Grant.

Not wanting to let a good crisis go to waste, religious right leaders like James Dobson, Jerry Falwell, Grant Jeffries, Hal Lindsey, Gary North, Pat Robertson and Jack Van Impe all got into the act, stoking the flames of hysteria in their sermons and rhetoric, this despite evidence of cooperation and progress between government and industry in dealing with the problem.

Still, many people were skeptical of the assurances and anxious about what would happen at midnight on January 1, 2001. And who could blame them with all the conflicting information about Y2K?

It sounded like a relatively simple problem requiring a relatively simple solution, but in fact demanded corrective action on an extensive global scale. If that action wasn't taken, systems would "break down." And what would be the consequences?

According to the more hysterical predictions, it was going to cause power outages, freeze assets, wipe out life savings or even compromise our strategic defenses. Cash registers wouldn't work, credit cards couldn't be swiped and a generation that couldn't perform simple mathematics without the aid of a calculator would be at a loss, thus jeopardizing commerce and collapsing the global economy.

Although mankind had managed to survive for thousands of years without computers, for some reason a digital meltdown suddenly meant the end of the world as we knew it.

Heeding the warnings and preferring to be safe than sorry, governments set up committees to ensure contingency planning and to monitor remedial efforts, especially those aimed at safeguarding critical infrastructures such as telecommunications and public utilities.

While I personally know people who cannot function without their smart phones or Blackberrys, it's hard to imagine all of civilization grinding to a complete halt without computers. The Amish, for example, seem to be doing okay without them.

But I digress …

For its part, the United States Government acted with a sense of urgency rarely seen in a bureaucracy by passing the Year 2000 Information and Readiness Disclosure Act in 1998. The measure called for cooperation between the public and private sector in tackling the Y2K problem and creating internal continuity of operations plans in case of trouble.

Coordinated out of the White House by the President's Council on Year 2000 Conversion, the effort was overseen by Council Chair John Koskinen and conducted with the assistance of the Federal Emergency Management Agency (FEMA) and an interim Critical Infrastructure Protection Group of the Department of Justice. As a part of the government's outreach program, several websites were created, including Y2K.gov. Each of the federal agencies involved in the effort had their own Y2K task forces that worked with private sector counterparts.

Fortunately, the international community was already a step

ahead of the U.S. The International Y2K Cooperation Center (IY2KCC) had been set up by representatives from more than 120 counties back in 1988. With funding from the World Bank, IY2KCC set up shop in Washington, D.C. in early 1999.

At the same time, tech departments worldwide got cracking by preparing for Y2K, spending billions of dollars upgrading their systems. Banks, for example, converted to full four-digit year entries on check forms to prevent accounting errors. Insurance companies offered coverage for business failure due to Y2K. Law firms prepared themselves for Y2K class action suits, and gun dealers and other survivalist-related businesses capitalized on the flourishing craze

Y2K also left its mark on multimedia. The publishing industry saw the proliferation of books on the subject, including Mark Joseph's *Deadline Y2K*. The Millennium Bug found its way into TV programs, comic strips and computer games. There was even an action movie entitled *Y2K: Year To Kill* released in 1999 with the tagline: "Those who prepared for the Millennium became the targets of those who didn't."

In all, preparations for Y2K cost more than 300 billion dollars. But apparently it was money well spent because – despite sporadic reported problems – January 1, 2000 came and went with scarcely a glitch, making it the most-hyped non-event of the Nervous Noughties.

However, suspicions still linger about the whole affair. Was Y2K the potential menace that we were led to believe or an elaborate attempt on the part of computer specialists and service providers to drum up business on the tail end of the Internet bubble? Or was it just a classic example of mass hysteria like that *War of the Worlds* broadcast back in 1938?

Whatever, the computer era has created a whole new venue of end-times mania. Of all forms of media that have exploited the apocalypse – Hollywood, the publishing industry, television – the most oversaturated source of Armageddon porn (also referred to as pessimism porn) has to be the Internet. In fact, the so-called Information Superhighway is one maddeningly intricate labyrinth of doom, gloom and paranoia – the rational thinking man's cyber vision of Hell.

Go to Google's search engine and type in the phrase "end of the world" and you'll get 782 *million* results (as of this writing). "End times" renders 488 million. "The apocalypse" 22 million and "Armageddon" 11.5 million. And that's just scratching the surface.

Want to waste several hours of your life? Go to YouTube and type in any of those phrases and take your pick of hundreds of amateur videos related to doomsday theories from obviously authoritative sources – perfect strangers with fertile imaginations and a lot of time on their hands.

Better yet, for a good laugh, sample some of the countless Web sites devoted to psychic predictions in which the fate of the world is often mingled with the future escapades of Hollywood's elite. You won't know what's worse – the prospect of a super volcano devastating the heartland of America or Angelina Jolie breaking the heart of Brad Pitt.

What – you might wonder – does someone have to gain (beside attention) from building a website devoted to such dubious content? Hits, of course! And, in some cases, a steady stream of advertising revenue for 1-800 psychic reading hotlines, self-promotion or as a recruitment tool for faith-based organizations like, for example, the Kingdom Voice Ministry and Impact Christian Books.com and the merchandise (books, CDs, DVDs) they have for sale.

The Internet has also become a battleground on which domestic and foreign governments, terrorists and political activists are either flirting with the idea of launching cyber attacks on their adversaries or have already launched a few salvos. According to a 2007 U.S. Pentagon report, Chinese military hackers have designed a detailed plan to disable America's aircraft battle carrier fleet in what would amount to an electronic Pearl Harbor.

In 2010, Wikileaks released U.S. State Department cables suggesting that Iran and Islamic hardliners in India also posed a cyber threat. Evidently, certain members of the Indian mujahedeen are real computer geeks who have been trained in wireless hacking techniques in support of terrorist attacks.

And speaking of WikiLeaks, its founder and serial whistleblower Julian Assange sent the U.S. government into a tizzy and sparked an international manhunt when he released more than a thousand American diplomatic cables in his possession in the fall of 2010.

Only six percent of the cables were classified as "secret" (40 percent were classified as "confidential"), but nonetheless proved highly embarrassing at the very least, especially those that indicated that U.S. officials were involved in diplomatic espionage. Thus began a new era in cyberspace in which the Information Superhighway became the Too Much Information Superhighway.

Assange's subsequent arrest in London on alleged Swedish sex charges provoked politically sympathetic hackers to attack U.S. corporate Websites. Proving their byte was worst than their bark, the cyber insurgents temporarily shut down Visa's and MasterCard's homepages and lead many to wonder what would happen if these activists, or the Chinese, or the Iranians were able to hack into the Strategic Air Command. Armageddon 2.0?

Whether these concerns are legitimate or not, it looks like they'll trigger another Y2K-like project costing billions in U.S. taxpayer dollars. Congress has already passed something called the Cybersecurity Enhancement Act with an Obama administration price tag of $12 billion. Critics of the measure contend that no one actually knows how much it will cost to achieve cybersecurity with estimates running as high as $50 billion in federal contracts.

On the bright side, this sort of ill-conceived and executed effort is just the shot in the arm the U.S. technology sector needs to lift it out of the doldrums. After all, it's only money and it's not like we haven't wasted more than that on certain unnecessary defense projects in the past.

Besides, you can't put a price on a sense of security – even a false one – can you?

CHAPTER 13

Gimme Shelter

"You can run, but you can't hide." – Joe Louis

IT'S A SIGN of the times … or a sign of timely hysteria: Fallout shelters are making a comeback.

Following the devastating Japanese earthquake in March 2011, sales of doomsday bunkers in the United States reportedly rose 1000 percent. In fact, as of this writing, a 137,000 square foot bunker – designed to accommodate 950 people for a year and capable of withstanding a 50-megaton nuclear blast – was being built beneath the grasslands of Nebraska.

Even before the Japanese disaster, sales of doomsday shelters were on the rise, according to a 2010 article in *USA Today*. For a mere minimum of $400,000, you too can have an underground shelter constructed on your property in the hope of protecting you and your loved ones from catastrophes such as nuclear attack, asteroid strikes or tsunamis – provided you have ample warning.

One Texas-based company called Radius Engineering has been manufacturing fiberglass underground shelters for several decades and claims that recent business is booming (no pun intended). The facilities can accommodate as few as 10 and up to 2000 people, providing up to five years of power, food, water and filtered area. In fact, Radius constructed and installed a $41-million dollar shelter that can house 750 people – but won't disclose who commissioned it or where the shelter is located.

Another article in *Popular Mechanics* reports that bomb-shelter technology hasn't changed much since the dawn of the Cold War. But the quality of modern fallout shelters has improved from the day of the crude backyard bunker. Now they're larger and more capable of withstanding an atom-splitting, earth-shattering event – as long as it's not located in the immediate radius of Ground Zero.

For instance, for $200 per square foot, you can fortify your house by having a ballistic "Level 8" hardened interior installed to withstand an assault from AK-47s. For $600 per square foot you can have an underground bunker attached to your house that even grenades can't penetrate. Talk about protecting yourself from a home invasion …

Up in Ontario, Canada a bomb-shelter builder named Bruce Beach has created the Ark Two Survival Community, a compound buried under 14 feet of soil. It comes equipped with a library, a conference room, a laundry room, a kitchen, day rooms and sleeping quarters – all the comforts of home in what is essentially a spacious mass grave. It accommodates about 150 people – if you call that accommodating.

A wise investment or a waste of money? That depends on how pessimistic you are about the current state of world and otherworldly affairs. The will to survive has always been strong in the human species. But one has to ask himself, if the worst happens and the world as we know it is reduced to a bleak wasteland of smoldering radioactive ruin, will survival be worth it?

And what if the outlook for the not so late, great planet Earth is far more positive? Well then, that's a mighty expensive underground rec room you've got there.

If you can't afford a six-figure underground shelter, how about a safe/panic room in your house? Although intended to provide sanctuary for you and your loved ones in the rare instance of a home invasion, this addition to your house could serve as a handy haven during a Category 4 hurricane or a medium-size earthquake. Of course, in the event of a nuclear holocaust, you and the "safe" room will get vaporized along with the rest of your house. But let's keep an open mind …

Safe rooms can be constructed for a more reasonable price of $8,000 (for one the size of a telephone booth) to $80,000 (for one the size of a bedroom). The door alone, usually bullet and entry-resistant with internal steel framing, could run you $20,000-$25,000 but, hey, that's the most important component. Walls are steel-studded, braced with additional reinforcing ties and faced with steel sheet or another bullet-resistant material, but can be covered with flame-retardant sheetrock, tile or other decorative finishes to give the room an appealing ambiance. Concrete floors are ideal, but you can go with wood as long as you add supplementary protection.

Of course, your safe room must also be outfitted with an exhaust system, multiple forms of communication with the outside world, and sound-proofed, not only to limit unwanted communication from attackers, but also to prevent intruders from your conversations. It should also be stocked with non-perishable food, bottle water and gas masks. And let's not forget a concealed camera located outside the room so you can see what's going on beyond the steel-framed door.

If we are to believe that fallout shelters and safe rooms are an effective survival option, it would appear that the rich, paranoid and mechanically gifted stand a better chance of inheriting a post-apocalyptic world. It certainly puts a new spin on the concept of survival of the fittest.

Although ongoing existence has been a top priority among humans since the days of the caveman, the roots of modern survivalism can be traced to the Great Depression of the 1930's. It was during this period that the need for preparedness was especially acute. Not only was the global economy in a shambles, but fascism and communism was on the rise, world war was inevitable, and natural disasters were always a possibility.

Of course, the movement got a significant boost with the development of nuclear weapons and the subsequent Cold War. In fact, one could say that its real hey day was in the "duck and cover" era of the 1950's and 1960's when public anxiety was at its height, spurred by ongoing conflict between the United States and Soviet Union that seemed to portend ultimate confrontation.

That apprehension wasn't alleviated by high-profile government Civil Defense programs that promoted public bomb shelters and personal fallout shelters, as well as nuclear "survival training" for grade school children. There isn't a baby boomer alive who doesn't look back on that time without a certain dark nostalgia.

It was during this period that survivalist literature started to gain a foothold in the public consciousness. Notably, there was Howard Ruff's 1974 book *Famine and Survival in America*, which offered advice on food storage and hoarding precious metals in anticipation of an economic collapse.

That was followed in 1975 by other survival-themed books and newsletters such as a monthly tabloid called *The Survivor*, which included editorials by Kurt Saxon and reprints of early American literature on frontier skills and crude technology. As a matter of fact, Saxon was among the first to use the term "survivalist" to identify those subscribed to the Boy Scout of motto of "be prepared."

In 1980, author John Pugsley published the *New York Times* bestseller *The Alpha Strategy*, now considered something of a bible for food and household supply hoarders convinced that rampant inflation and shortages are the wave of the future. A renewed arms race between the United States and the soon-to-be defunct Soviet Union in that decade also prompted the creation of the first survivalist magazine called (of all things) *Survive*. Edited by science fiction writer Jerry Pournelle, *Survive* has done just that – now incarnated as an online blog with the tagline, "For those of us who won't just lay down and die."

The survivalist movement got another shot in the arm in the 1990's when Y2K fears reached fever pitch. Predictions of power outages and food and gasoline shortages goosed the sales of books such as *The Hippy Survival Guide to Y2K* by Mike Oehler and *Boston on*

Surviving Y2K by Boston T. Party. Although the turn of the millennium proved uneventful, it was shortly followed by the terrorist attacks of September 11, 2001, which only gave survivalists more reason to believe the collapse of civilization was imminent.

More recently, the worldwide Web has become a social club for millions of self-described survivalists. Among the most popular sites and blogs that cater to these latter-day Jeremiah Johnsons are:

- SurvivalRing (www.survivalring.org) – a set of Web sites focused on preparedness education.
- Off Grid Survival (www.offgridsurvival.com) – a site that serves as a resource for people interested in survival topics and "off the grid" living.
- Conspiracy Café.Net (www.conspiracycafe.net) – a message board where conspiracy theorists can let their suspicions run wild.
- Survivalist Boards.com (http://www.survivalistboards.com/) – a forum for discussion on all things related to survivalism.
- The Survivalist Blog.net (www.thesurvivalistblog.net) – a site where the tagline says it all: Live Better, Live Cheaper … Survive When Things Get Tough.

Besides providing a virtual town hall meeting place for like-minded survivalists, many of these sites also include a catalogue of products capable of sustaining a small army during the worst of times. A typical survivalist checklist might include:

- Long shelf life food
- First aid kits
- Survival kits
- Water filters, distillers, purification and storage
- Cooking, heating and lighting
- Camping products
- Radio, communications and electrical/electronic devices

- Other items such as solar powered equipment, power sources, lights and lanterns, safety items and instructional books.

The survivalist movement has also given rise to a budding business opportunity known as food insurance. For about $200 a pop, you can order an emergency food supply kit of freeze-dried entrees that will provide three meals per day to one adult for two weeks. The rationale for this precaution is that you never know when a hurricane, tornado or other act of God will strike.

Celebrity spokespersons like Glenn Beck have taken it a step further, suggesting that with the country going to hell in a hand basket and a financial meltdown looming on the horizon, it only makes sense to stock up on chow. Of course, the time to buy and store the food is before the feces hit the fan. Otherwise, you might have a problem with home delivery.

As vendors such as Food Insurance.com point out, frozen foods bought in a supermarket require low temperature storage conditions and will thaw and spoil soon after the power shuts down. Dehydrated canned foods are shelf-stable, but lose their nutritional content over time. Freeze-dried foods like the stuff produced for the military and NASA, on the other hand, can last up to 10 years without spoiling. But do the math – it would take 260 kits at a total price of $52,000 just to feed one adult for a decade. What happens after that expiration date is not clear, but considering that radioactivity can last for centuries, you've got to wonder how viable it is to hoard food.

And don't forget the automatic weapons and ammo. If all hell breaks loose, you'll want to be packing because other survivors certainly will and may not be as peace-loving and selfless as you. Provisions won't do you much good if you can't protect them from looters and marauders. So gun manufacturers aren't just marketing to hunters and security conscious citizens, they're also targeting survivalists.

And apparently with much success. Although no one knows exactly how many guns there are in the United States, the Federal

Bureau of Investigation estimates that about 4.5 million legal guns are sold in the United States each year. And the average gun owner has at least four of them.

Fear has always been a compelling reason to stock up. So it comes as no surprise that in a volatile and often violent world, many cling to the flimsy hope that an underground annex, an arsenal of weapons and a year's supply of rations will see them through a societal collapse – if not an extinction level event.

Ultimately, it comes down to a blue state versus red state perspective: Those who would rather beat their swords into ploughshares can only look upon the survivalist industry as an enabler of the lunatic fringe, while vigilant survivalists believe they will have the last laugh. But if worse comes to worst, is anyone going to feel like laughing?

CHAPTER 14

Game Over

"The best way to predict the future is to create it." – *Peter F. Drucker*

NO STROLL DOWN Desolation Row would be complete without a foray into the virtual world of apocalyptic and post-apocalyptic video games. For it is there – in a fantasy wasteland of rubble, toxic nuclear fallout, and marauding, flesh-eating mutants – that one can vicariously experience the aftermath of an Armageddon that stubbornly refuses to come to pass and emerge relatively unscathed.

Of all the obsessions in modern pop culture, perhaps none is more addictive and all-consuming than video gaming. Whether played online, in the privacy of one's home, or on mobile units while in transit, these mesmerizing diversions have become the cultural crack of malleable minds.

Just how popular are these games? According to the International Data Corporation, gaming was a $26.6 billion worldwide industry in 2006. U.S. video game hardware sales alone totaled $6.6 billion in 2007, while software sales totaled 15.8 billion. And although sales dipped during the recessionary years from 2008-2011, 72% of people between the ages of six and 44 in the U.S. play video games, and the number of American households that play them is expected to increase to 80% by 2012. By 2014, the video game industry is projected to be three times the size of the music industry, raking in some $84 billion per year.

Major manufacturers of video game consoles include:

- Microsoft – whose Xbox 360 sold 46.3 million units as of 2010;
- Sony – whose Playstation 3 and PSP (Playstation Portable device) sold 40.1 million units; and
- Nintendo – with 74.4 million units of its Wii console and Nintendo DS portable service sold.

What began roughly 40 years ago as simple, harmless fare with the likes of Pong, Pac-Man and Donkey Kong has rapidly evolved – or devolved, as the case may be – into sophisticated simulator training exercises in mass murder and mayhem. The very fact that video games now come with their own parental rating code says a lot about an industry that makes its profit by exploiting our base instincts and inherent bloodlust.

At first glance, it's hard to understand why anyone would want to escape to the grim, dreary dreamscape that is the typical doomsday video game. But once embedded in its dystopian scenario, the motivation becomes more apparent. *It's only a game*, one rationalizes. Therefore, where's the harm in some imaginary stalking, hunting and slaughter in a make-believe world of kill or be killed?

Before we delve into specific examples of this phenomenon, a crash course in some basic industry jargon and acronyms is in order:

- **RPG** stands for **role-playing game**. In all RPGs players assume the part of a specific character and control many of that character's actions.
- **MMO** (or **MMOG**) is short for **massively multiplayer online (game)**, which is capable of supporting hundreds or thousands of players simultaneously.
- **MMORPG** refers to **massively multiplayer online role-playing**

game, a genre of RPGs in which a large number of players interact within a virtual game world that continues to exist and evolve even while the player is offline.

- MMORPGs are a worldwide phenomenon. In 2008, Western consumer spending on subscription MOOPGs reached $1.4 billion. *World of Warcraft*, a popular MMORPG, had more than 11 million subscribers as of March, 2011.
- **A first-person shooter** – is a video game that centers play on gun and projectile weapon-based combat through the eyes of a protagonist.

Okay, now that we've got that straight, back to bedlam …

A perusal of some of the more noteworthy doomsday video games (as evaluated by the *U.K. Guardian*) may shed some light on where our collective consciousness has drifted in the post-Cold War era. These include:

Wasteland (Interplay, 1988) – The player's mission is to lead a group of survivalists on a journey though a desolate landscape while fending off attacking mutants. This was considered a groundbreaker in its time in terms of character customization and upgrade systems. It was also seen as a precursor to the wildly popular Fallout series.

Midwinter (1989) – Set in 2099 A.D., this game takes place on an island during nuclear winter following a cataclysmic meteorite strike in 2040. The objective is to recruit 32 people to oppose the invasion of an evil military force. Viewed as a landmark in open-world design, the game spawned a sequel, Midwinter II: Flames of Freedom.

Beneath a Steel Sky (Revolution, 1994) – Boasting a visual design from Watchmen artist Dave Gibbons, this game has a Mad Max flavor to it. Although no specific time period is given, it is obvious the story takes place in a future where the Earth has been ravaged by either pollution or nuclear fallout. The player guides an orphaned boy from the Australian outback to a totalitarian metropolis ruled by an omnipotent computer network.

Deus Ex (Ion Storm, 2000) – In the 2050s, mankind has been virtually wiped out by a deadly pandemic. But there is a cure called Ambrosia. That's the good news. The bad news is that it's the sole property of a military stratocracy and your assignment – should you choose to accept it (and why wouldn't you if you went to the trouble of buying this game?) – is to assume the role of a nanotech-augmented United Nations Anti-Terrorist Coalition agent named JC Denton, travel the world and combat a variety of conspiratorial organizations. Yes, it's that intricate.

Half-Life 2 (Valve, 2004) – The human race is enslaved by the evil Combine in this award-winning sequel to … (what else?) **Half-Life**. Five years in the making at a production cost of $40 million, the game revolves around the exploits of a character named Gordon Freeman who faces a diverse set of enemies with various types of weapons and methods of attack. One of the game's many set pieces includes an excursion to a mining town populated by zombies.

Phantom Dust (Microsoft Game Studios Japan, 2003) – This adventure takes place on a devastated Earth covered with a deadly dust that has driven most survivors into underground caverns. There are four aspects of gameplay which include interaction, arsenal building, mission assignment within the underground city, and combat in multiple arenas on the planet's surface. Up to four players can wage battle on split screens using the same console or over Xbox Live.

S.T.A.L.K.E.R: Shadow of Chernobyl (GSC Game World, 2007) – In this aptly-titled first person shooter, the player is a mercenary in a stark, post-nuclear Ukrainian wasteland following a second Chernobyl explosion (as if the first one wasn't bad enough). You're battling vicious radioactive monsters and bucking the odds on various suicide missions for the sake of some raggedy survivors. Which I suppose is still better than spending a weekend at an Orlando theme park.

Left 4 Dead (Valve, 2008) – Like any number of George Romero-inspired zombie movies, this game has you shooting, stabbing and bludgeoning your way through the Keystone State besieged by the living dead. Set during the aftermath of the "Green Flu" pandemic, four immune protagonists must cooperate to overcome hordes of psychotic, rabid humans. Kind of like being a public school teacher.

Fallout 3 (Betheseda 2008) – It's 200 years after the nuclear devastation of America and you're celebrating the Bicentennial by escaping the safety of Vault 101, a survival shelter, and embarking on a rescue mission through the ruins of Washington, D.C., now known as Capital Wasteland. The person you're trying to save is your Dad. And, no, he's not a federal employee with a lucrative pension. Along the way you'll be battling a myriad of pesky enemies – former lobbyists no doubt.

Metro 2033 (THQ, 2010) – This first-person shooter takes place in post-apocalyptic Moscow, but your nemesis is not Vlad ("the Impaler") Putin, the KGB or the Politburo. Rather, you're up against swarms of mutants and hostile humans known as the Dark Ones. Most of the mayhem takes place in the city's metro (like it does on any given weekday in the New York subway system), but missions occasionally take place above ground. Either way, you're loaded for Russian bear.

Fallen Earth (K2 Network, 2009) – If you're looking for a welcome change of scenery, this free-to-play MMO takes place around the Grand Canyon. That's where an investment tycoon named Brenhauer has established a self-sufficient economic and military mini-state after a series of natural disasters have fallen the United States. The Earth is then devastated by a pandemic and nuclear conflict. As a result, the Hoover Dam Garrison and Grand Canyon Province have become the last vestiges of human civilization – and the battleground of warring factions that include those intent on restoring the old world order, those seeking to build a new world in their own image, and those happily devoted to chaos and anarchy. Any resemblance to the Kardashians is purely coincidental.

Rage (id Software, 2011) – On August 23, 2009, the Apophis asteroid strikes the Earth, wiping out 99.9% of mankind. But not to worry – the 0.1 percenters (VIPs) have been safely buried underground in cryogenic pads called Arks in order to rebuild civilization. The player, however, wakes 106 years later to find that he is the only survivor of his heavily damaged Ark and, after reaching the surface, embarks on a perilous journey that pits him against an assortment of post-apocalyptic bandits and mutants in what may best be described as the Wild West meets Mad Max.

Fall Out: New Vegas (Bethesda Softworks, 2010) – This latest sequel to the lucrative Fallout franchise takes place in a retro-futuristic Sin City long after Wayne Newton has left town – some 200 years after the Great War of 2077 to be exact. In the role of The Courier, the player has been shot and left for dead in a shallow grave, but rescued by a robot and rehabilitated. He then renews his quest to retrieve a stolen package and deliver it to New Vegas, battling his way through the Mojave Desert. If only the U.S. Postal Service was as efficient.

And that's just the tip of the iceberg. There are dozens of other apocalyptic/post-apocalyptic games just like these – each one more graphically violent than the next.

I suppose one should be thankful that gamers have these scenarios to keep them occupied instead of being on the streets stealing hub caps, hacking into online accounts or otherwise being gainfully employed. It does, however, say something less than flattering about our values as a society – and something disheartening about human nature overall.

Some pseudo-psychologists maintain that video games of this nature serve a useful purpose, that there are positive aspects that outweigh the negative. Such activity strengthens hand and eye coordination, they tell us – which I suppose is a good thing, essential to the increasing demands of today's multitasking social environment. Others have floated the notion that first-person shooters are honing necessary survival skills, which should come in handy if and when World Wars III, IV and Z come to past.

But with each new generation of RPGs, the graphics are becoming increasingly authentic to the point where discernible illusion is gradually giving way to an alternate reality. The danger is that impressionable minds are becoming desensitized to the grim actuality of death and destruction, thus ensuring the perpetuation of armed conflict as a viable solution – as opposed to a necessary evil.

That's why these games come with parental guidance warning ratings. Of course, that hasn't prevented them from being perennial holiday stocking stuffers.

But hey, forget about Christmas – our apparent obsession with apocalyptic video games reveals a curious societal death wish. It's as if adolescents, young adults and parents alike *can't wait for Armageddon*.

As Aesop warned, be careful what you wish for.

CHAPTER 15

Have the Mayans Ever Lied to You?

"The only way to profitably predict the future is to accurately understand history." – Aaron Wall

AS OF THIS writing, none of the countless predictions of apocalyptic reckoning made over the past 2,000 years have come to pass.

Every date associated with impending doom has proven uneventful – even in a world of nuclear proliferation and geological and meteorological volatility, even in a solar system that has been described as a shooting gallery of sitting duck planets and wayward comets and asteroids.

But wait! There's still a date on the calendar that surely portends the end of the world as we know it … December 21, 2012.

Consider the numerical oddity of the date - 12/21/12. That has to mean *something*, doesn't it? And the fact that the Mayan calendar *ends* on that date must have significance. What else could it foreshadow but the end of days?

Actually, it doesn't mean much of anything and you can see why when you delve a bit into the history of the Mayans and separate fact from fiction about their impressive yet cockamamie calendar.

Mayan civilization began approximately 4,000 years ago and spawned a modest empire that spanned the better part of what is now Central America from the southern states of Mexico through

Guatemala, Belize, El Salvador and part of Honduras. During its Classic Period (circa 250 AD – 900 AD), it was an advanced culture for its time in that its people possessed a gift for writing and extraordinary architectural skills. As today's Mayan ruins attest, it was a society noted for its great pyramids and other examples of sophisticated urban design. The Mayans also had other talents – they were masters of astronomy and creators of complex and remarkably accurate calendars.

The Mayans thought of time as an interweaving of spiritual cycles. These cycles served practical purposes when it came to planning agricultural, commercial and administrative tasks, but they also contained a highly religious significance. In fact, each day was represented by a patron spirit and had a specific use.

Circa 238 B.C., someone indigenous to Mesoamerica – not necessarily a Mayan – used the Tzolkin (a sacred 260-day almanac) and the Haab (a 365-day secular calendar) to approximate the date when the world began. That date corresponded to August 11, 3114 B.C. on the Gregorian calendar. Next, the Tzolkin and the Haab were combined to create a cycle of 52 years which was dubbed the Calendar Round. Of course, this system precluded the ability to record an historic date older than 52 years. But the Mayans came up with a way to solve this problem, and here's where things get interesting …

The Mayans expanded on the 52-year Calendar Round by devising a longer calendar called the "Long Count," lasting 5,126 years. The base year for the Long Count began at 0.0.0.0.0. Each zero went from 0-19 and each represented a tally of days. In other words, the first day of the Long Count was 0.0.0.0.1. After 19 days, the date moved up to the next level – 0.0.0.1.0 – for the 20th day and so on. It would reach 0.0.1.0.0 in approximately one year, 0.1.0.0.0 in about 20 years, and 1.0.0.0.0 in approximately 400 years.

Here's the thing: It has long been the assumption of many wishful Doomsday devotees that something cataclysmic will happen when the Mayan Long Count calendar runs out. What they are basing this assumption on is unclear, but it seems to hinge on the fact that the

Mayans used the numbers 13 and 20 as the root of their numerical systems. Even then, experts are divided over whether the calendar will end as of 13.0.0.0.0 or 20.0.0.0.0. Those who believe the former maintain that 13.0.0.0.0 represents a period of 5126 years. And, since the Long Count started on 0.0.0.0.0, which corresponds to the modern date of August 11, 3114 BC, it would appear that the Mayan Long Count ends on December 21, 2012.

Of course, the Calendar could continue to 20.0.0.0.0. But that would delay the Day of Reckoning considerably and no one is going to buy a book that warns of an Apocalypse approximately 2800 years in the future. Besides, December 21 marks the winter solstice (not to mention four shopping days until Christmas) and that must have some sort of mystical significance.

Sure enough, the sun will be aligned with the center of the Milky Way for the first time in 26,000 years on December 21, 2012. So there's your "proof" that a great cosmic event – reminiscent of the infamous Jupiter Effect -- will occur on that day.

But then the so-called experts can't even agree whether it will be a bad or happy event. Some are predicting global devastation, while others are downplaying expectations by envisaging a new age of enlightenment. Assurances by learned and rational members of the scientific community that nothing significant will happen on December 21, 2012 are currently falling on deaf ears. After all, where's the fun in predicting that the world *won't* end?

Ironically, the ancient Mayans had an apocalypse of their own long before their calendar was scheduled to end. In the 16th century, Spanish conquistadors laid waste to their kingdom, slaughtering or enslaving countless numbers of Maya and looting their treasures. In fact, the violent dismantling of the Mayan empire gave rise to the myth that these resourceful indigenous people subsequently disappeared from the face of the Earth – embellishing the notion they were a mystical cult with a supernatural perception of the ways of the universe.

Tell that to the seven million Maya who live today near the areas in which they flourished some 15,000 years ago – along the Yucatan

Peninsula, in Guatemala, Honduras, El Salvador and Belize. Ask them what they think about the 2012 doomsday theories and they'll no doubt tell you to go jump into the Gulf of Mexico. In fact, they mockingly but aptly refer to the 2012 scare as "the gringo invention."

So what exactly do the doomsday believers think will happen on December 21, 2012? Let us count the crackpot theories:

- **Daffy Doomsday Prediction #1: Geomagnetic reversal of the North and South magnetic poles.**

Some envision a sudden shift in the Earth's axis caused by a solar maximum (flare) and resulting in a cataclysmic global earthquake. Mountains will crumble and sky-high tsunamis will engulf the major cities in the world as well as everything else in their path.

Why it won't happen: There is no scientific evidence linking a solar maximum to a geomagnetic reversal. Even if there were, a polar shift takes up to 7,000 years to complete and wouldn't start on a particular, predictable date. The Earth's magnetic field periodically reverses its polarity, but the last time it happened was about 780,000 years ago. And there is no evidence that a magnetic field reversal has ever caused a biological extinction.

- **Daffy 2012 Doomsday Prediction #2: The Earth will suffer the consequences of a massive solar storm.**

In the wake of solar flares in August, 2010, a number of media outlets reported that a source at NASA warned that the phenomenon was merely a precursor to a greater solar flare that had the potential to fry the world's power grid.

Why I wouldn't worry about it if I were you: The same media worry warts report that similar solar storms caused "worldwide chaos" in 1821 and 1859 – when some telegraph wires were disrupted. This time around, warns a report by the National Academy of Sciences, we could be hit by a blast with the equivalent energy of 100 million hydrogen bombs, causing "1 to 2 trillion dollars in damages to society's high-tech infrastructure" and requiring four to 10 years for recovery.

And when is this due? Possibly in 2012 or 2013. The timing's right, but is the *potential* disruption of your GPS cause for global panic? Sounds like Y2K all over again.

- **Daffy 2012 Doomsday Prediction #3: Planet X (aka Nibiru) will collide with or pass closely by Earth.**

A collision with this wayward mass from beyond Neptune would completely destroy our planet and a close shave would result in massive tidal waves.

Why this is poppycock: First of all, it sounds like this theory was inspired by the aforementioned scenario of *When Worlds Collide*. Second, this event was originally predicted for 2003 – and nothing happened. Third, and most important, astronomers have universally concluded that Planet X – which was only a hypothesis to begin with – does not exist. This was confirmed with gravitational data gathered by the Voyager 2 space probe in 1989.

- **Daffy 2012 Doomsday Prediction #4: The Earth will be incinerated by a supernova.**

Specifically, the red supergiant star Betelgeuse (not to be confused with the Michael Keaton movie character Bettlejuice), which is due to explode.

Why they've got to be kidding: There's no way of predicting when Betelgeuse will reach supernova status to within 100,000 years. What's more, to threaten Earth a supernova would need to be no further than 25 light years from our solar system. Betelgeuse is some 600 light years away. So forget about it.

And while you're at it, you can disregard a similar warning that Alcyone, the largest star in the Pleiades cluster, is moving perilously close to our neighborhood. In fact, it's getting further away … like 400 light years.

- **Daffy 2012 Doomsday Prediction #5: We're about to be invaded by aliens.**

The Roswell incident in 1947, the U.S. military's mysterious Area 51 and subsequent UFO sightings and reports of alien abductions all add up to an impending attack by malevolent beings from beyond our solar system.

Why this is batshit crazy: Do we really need to go there?

And then there's 99942 Apophis, a near-Earth asteroid about 1000 feet across that is due to come in close proximity to our planet in 2013. Although Apophis isn't expected to pose a threat to Earth until at least 2036 (and even then the odds of impact are 1 in 250,000), that probably won't stop a chorus of Cassandras who'll suggest otherwise in the run-up to December 21.

The catastrophic possibilities associated with the end of the Mayan calendar have already been exploited to the hilt. In the blockbuster movie *2012*, the world was subjected to a smorgasbord of natural disasters – a volcanic eruption at Yellowstone Park; the San Andreas fault line splitting, sending California crumbling into the Pacific Ocean; global earthquakes targeting all the major landmarks; and colossal tsunamis engulfing New York, Washington, D.C. and mainland China. In short, an apocalyptic orgy of death, destruction and bad acting.

Between now and December 21, 2012 you can expect more of this kind of Armageddon porn from a legion of opportunistic producers, publishers and perennial purveyors of doom. And if all goes according to marketing plan, the apocalyptic overkill will make Y2K look like a picnic in comparison. So brace yourself.

The lunatic fringe of today's mass media has already surpassed the Spanish conquistadors as the primary looters of Mayan culture – and all for the sake of making a fast buck. There are approximately

250 books about 2012, the Mayan calendar and the end of the world based predominantly on groundless speculation currently offered at Amazon.com. So far, there have also been 55 movies and TV programs devoted to the subject. And a Google search renders approximately 1.74 *million* results.

But the good news is that the end may truly be in sight. Not for the world as we know it, but for Maya mania and the cult of personal destruction.

December 21, 2012 represents the last stand for the profit-making prophets of doom. If that date comes and goes without so much as a whimper, much less a bang, the public's interest in all things apocalyptic – and their patience with false prophets – will be seriously depleted if not utterly exhausted.

And as far as this skeptic is concerned, that day cannot come soon enough.

CHAPTER **16**

World Without End, Amen
(or What If They Gave an Apocalypse and Nobody Came?)

"It's the end of the world as we know it, and I feel fine." – R.E.M.

LET ME GO out on a limb here and make a bold prediction of my own – the world as we know it will *not* end on December 21, 2012.

There, it's on record.

If I'm right – and I believe I am – I will claim bragging rights as a better prophet than Edgar Cayce, Jeane Dixon, Hal Lindsey or even Criswell Predicts.

If I'm wrong – well, then it won't matter, will it?

The thing is, no one knows for sure where we're headed – certainly not those doomsday profiteers who are basing their predictions on convoluted Biblical and pseudo-scientific conjecture. Yet, too many of us are so willing to believe the worst will happen – oh we of little faith in humanity. We keep waiting for the axe to fall – and waiting and waiting. Perhaps it's time to set aside our fears, superstitions and innate fatalism and take a deep breath.

Why am I so convinced otherwise? Because in spite of a few close calls, we have managed to avoid nuclear war for some 66 years. This despite the fact that nine nations (the United States, Russia, China, the United Kingdom, France, India, Pakistan, Israel and North Korea) are known or believed to have nuclear weapons.

What is restraining these nations – some outright adversaries

– from using these weapons? Knowledge of the consequences. Given the choice between annihilation of the human race and coexistence made tolerable by relative wealth, our governments have chosen the comfort of materialism. Money it seems is not only the root of all evil, but also a pretty good incentive for civility and survival.

Never mind our financial institutions – Planet Earth is too big to fail. To paraphrase Gordon Gekko in the movie, *Wall Street*: Greed is good. It's good in that it is a powerful deterrent to nuclear annihilation, environmental negligence and economic collapse through financial malfeasance. In other words, mankind has a vested interest in avoiding a man-made apocalypse.

We've come too far to simply self-destruct whether by global warfare or manmade afflictions, which leaves only a natural cataclysm as the primary danger – and one that, with the help of science and technology, can be anticipated and dealt with – if not avoided – for the foreseeable future. In fact, the odds of an extinction-level event within the next million years – much less the next 100 years – are extremely low. That's a long time – well beyond the lifetimes of our children and our children's children. Long enough for mankind to put its knowledge, creativity and resourcefulness to better use than dwelling on death and destruction.

Having said that, here's another prediction you can take to the bank – one day, the world as we know it *will indeed* come to an end.

Precisely when that will happen, however, and how it will happen cannot be estimated with any certainty. Perhaps it will occur sooner rather than later. Perhaps it's just a matter of years or decades. Perhaps it will take centuries or several more eons. The cause may well be an all-out nuclear war ... or drastic climate change ... or some as of yet unknown virus ... or a sudden shift of the Earth's axis ... or the collision of our planet with a killer comet or asteroid ... or maybe, just maybe a massive solar flare. But eventually – it will happen.

But one thing's for sure – the exact time and nature of our planet's demise will not be envisioned in a crystal ball or spotted on an astrological chart. Nor will it follow the precise pattern of an ancient prophecy based on primitive superstition or a scenario conceived by an opportunistic movie studio executive. If foreseen at all, hopefully it will be through the clear eyes of a wiser, more enlightened generation that will accept its fate with grace and dignity.

There's no denying that we live in a troubled and perilous world. We are certainly at the mercy of a universe whose mysteries we have hardly begun to fathom. But the last thing we need right now is another book, movie, pamphlet or sermon that manipulates our darkest fears for not so petty profit.

One day, we may finally realize that while doom and gloom sells for some, there's nothing in it for the rest of us. Until then – and while there's still a buck to be made – numerous hucksters, charlatans and doomsday fatalists will continue to wallow in what amounts to a perverse and fruitless exercise in celebrating death instead of life. Time and time again they have predicted disaster – and time and time again they've been wrong. Whether you choose to join their ranks or focus instead on building a positive future is entirely up to you.

My advice? Don't fear the reaper come December 21, 2012 ... or on December 22, 23 or thereafter. Instead, get a life and enjoy the limited time allotted to you.

As Franklin Delano Roosevelt so famously declared, "We have nothing to fear but fear itself." And maybe not even that.

Notes

Chapter 1: Party Like It's 999

Edward P. Wallner, "The Year 1000 A.D. and the Millenial Panic," The NESS, July, 1998, http://www.theness.com/the-year-1000-1-d-and-the-millenial-panic/.

"Predictions for the End of the World From 999 to 1600," Trivia-Library.com, http://www.trvia-library.com/b/predictions-for-the-end-of-the-world-from-999-to-1600.html.

"Medieval End of the World Hoaxes," Museum of Hoaxes.com, http://www.museumofhoaxes.com/hoax/Hoaxipedia/Medieval_End_of_the_World_Hoaxes/.

Chapter 2: 'Cause The Bible Tells Me So

Genesis 6-9, The Holy Bible, edited by Reverend John P. O'Connell, The Catholic Press, Inc.

Genesis 19, Ibid.

Thessalonians 2, Ibid.

"How Seventh-day Adventists View Roman Catholicism," http://www.adventist,org/beliefs/statements/main_stat42.html.

Chapter 3: Seer Suckers

Gaia Reel, "It's The End of The World as We Know It: Previous Predictions of the end at Were a Bit Off," http://netowne.com/historical/glboal/theend.html

"Prophecies of St. Malachy – Concerning the Popes," http://ad2004.com/prophecy truths/Articles/Prophecy/Malacy.html.

"220 Dates for the End of the world," http://www.bible.ca/pre-date-setters.html.

Mother Shipton's Prophecies, http://www/pyramidtlc.org/mother/html.

The Amazing Criswell, http://en.wikipedia.org/wiki/The_Amazing_Criswell.

Criswell Predicts, The A.V. Club, http://www.avclub.com/articles/criswell_predicts,1370/

Maurice Woodruff, http://en.wikipedia.org/wiki/Maurice_Woodruff.

Joseph Bayly, What About Horoscopes, Chapter 2, http://www.ccel.us/bayly.ch2.html.

Chapter 4: The Nostradamus Spin Zone

Erika Cheetham, The Prophecies of Nostradamus (New York, G.P. Putnam's Sons, 1974).

Ward, Charles, The Oracles of Nostradamus (Modern Library, 1940.)

Hogue, John, Nostradamus: The Complete Prophecies (Element Books Limited, 1997).

Robert Stricklin, "Nostradamus and the Papal Succession," Gnostica, No. 49, Dec. 1978- Jan. 1979, pp 2-3.

Chapter 5: The Mighty Cayce Has Struck Out

York, Michael, *The Emerging Network: A Sociology of the New Age and Neo-Pagan Movements* (Rowman & Littlefield, 1995), p.60.

Gardner, Martin, *Fads & Fallacies In The Name Of Science* (Dover Publications, 1957), p.216-219.

Cerminara, Dr. Gona (1999), "The Medical Clairvoyance of Edgar Cayce." *Many Mansions*, pp. 13-15.

Auken, John Van (2005), *Edgar Cayce on the Revelation*. (Sterling, 2005).

Miller, Timothy. *American Alternative Religion*. (SUNY Press, 1995), p.354.

Bro, Harmon Hartzell. "Edgar C aye: A Seer out of Season," *Aquarian Press*, London, 1990.

Chapter 6: The Prime of Ms. Jeane Dixon

Montgomery, Ruth, *A Gift of Prophecy*. (Bantam Books, 1965.)

Jeane Dixon, Rene Noorbergen. *Jeane Dixon: My Life and Prophecies*. (William Morrow and Company, Inc., 1969).

David St. Albin Greene, "The Untold Story ...of Jeane Dixon," *National Observor*, 27 Oct. 1972.

Denis Brain, *Jeane Dixon: The Witnesses*, (Doubleday & Company, 1976), p147-148.

Carroll, Robert T. "Jeane Dixon & the Jeane Dixon effect." *The Skeptics Dictionary*. http://skepdic.com/dixon.html.

Betz, Paul (Ed.), Carnes, Mark (Ed.), *American National Biography: Supplement I (American National Biography Supplement)*, (Oxford University Press, 2002), pp.163-164.

Chapter 7: Hollywood Babble On

Internet Movie Database, http://www.imdb.com.

Worldwide Grosses, Box Office Mojo, http://www.boxofficemojo.com/alltime/world/

Chapter 8: Will The Real Antichrist Please Stand Up?

Armstrong, Herbert W. "Who Is The Beast?" Worldwide Church of God, 1960.

Chapter 9: Apocalypse When?

"220 Dates for the End of the world," http://www.bible.ca/pre-date-setters.html. Daniel 7-11, The Holy Bible, edited by Reverend John P. O'Connell, The Catholic Press, Inc. Hal Lindsay, Carole C. Carlson. *The Late, Great Planet Earth.* (Zondervan, 1970).

Skolfield, Ellis. "An End-Time Myth." Fishhouseministries.com/pdf/An-End-Time-Myth.pdf.

Stricklin, Robert. "Profits of Doom." American Atheist. Vol. 24, No.1, March, 1982. Pp. 24-25.

Chapter 10: Let Us Prey

"220 Dates for the End of the world," http://www.bible.ca/pre-date-setters.html. Sahagun, Louis. "End Times Religious Groups Want Apocalypse Soon." Los Angeles Times, USA. June 22, 2006.

Campion, Nardi Reeder. Ann the Word: The Life of Mother Ann Lee, Founder of the Shakers.(Little, Brown and Company, 1976).

Chapter 11: No Profit Left Behind

Catholic Answers Special Report: False Profit: Money, Prejudice, and Bad Theology in Time LaHaye's Left Behind Series.

Left Behind Series, Leftbehind.com Official Website of the Book Series.

John Cloud and Rancho Mirage. "Meet the Prophet." Time. June 23, 2002.

Gribben, Crawford. Writing the Rapture: Prophecy Fiction in Evangelical America. (Oxford University Press, 2009).

Leung, Rebecca. "Rise of the Righteous Army." 60 Minutes-CBS News. http://www.cbsnews.com/stories/2004/02/05/60minutes/main598218.shtml.

Chapter 12: Et Tu, Y2K?

Carrington, Damian (2000-01-04). "Was Y2K bug a boost?" BBC News/

White House shifts Y2K focus to states, CNN (Feb. 23, 1999).

FCC Y2K Communications Sector Report (March 1999) copy available at WUTCPDF.

Federal Communications Commission Spearheads Oversight of the U.S. Communications Industries' Y2K Preparedness, Wiley, Rein & Fielding Fall 1999.

Y2K: Overhyped and oversold? Report from BBC News, Jan. 6, 2000.

"The Y2K crisis that never happened: Part 2." Religious Tolerance. http://www.religioustolerance.org/y2k_probl1.htm.

Steele, Robert David. "America's Cyber Scam." Homeland Security Today. Feb. 8, 2010. http://www.hstoday.us/content/view/12094/151/.

Cyber-attacks could cause global 'catastrophe.'" The Telegraph. http://www.telegraph.co.uk/technology/news/8262628/Cyber-attacks-could-cause-global-catastrophe.html.

"China's cyberwarfare capabilities grow." MSNBC.com. http://www.msnbc. com/id/33439397/ns/technology_and-science-security/

Chapter 13: Gimme Shelter

Matheny, Keith. "Doomsday shelters making a comeback." USA Today. Retrieved 8/29/2010.

"Going underground? Sales of spaces in U.S. doomsday bunker soar 1000% after Japan quake awakens nuclear fallout fears." Daily Mail, Apr.1, 2011.

"Food Storage," Gospel Library. The Church of Jesus Christ of Latter-day Saints. Retrieved 1/11/2011. Kurt Saxon. "What Is A Survivalist?" (http:// www.textfiles.com.survival.whatsurv). Retrieved 1/11/2011.

"$50 and Up Underground House Book: Underground Housing and Shelter." (http://www.undergroundhousing.com/book.html). Retrieved 1/11/2011.

Williams, Alex (2008-04-06). "Duck and Cover: It's the New Survivalism," (nttp://wwww.nytimes.com/2008/04/06/fashion/06survival.html?_ r=1&oref=slogin). *The New York Times*. Retrieved 1/11/2011.

Emergency Preparedness and Survival Products from B&A Products. http:// www.baproducts.com/emerprep.htm.

Freeze dried foods. Foodinsurance.com. http://www.foodinsurance.com/ freeze_dried_food/freeze_dried-food.php.

Chapter 14: Game Over

"The ten greatest post-apocalyptic video games." The Guardian, retrieved 8/31/2011.

"Is gaming a real industry?" Baylor University, School of Engineering Computer Science, www.ecs.baylor,edu/compouter_science/index.php?id=44304

"PC Gamer's top 100 PC Games of all time." *PC Gamer*. February 5, 2010.

"U.S. video industry growth seen slowing," Reuters, January 5, 2008.

Video Games, Wiki Analysis, www.wikinvest.com/industry/Video_Games.

Bettinson, Mat. "PC gaming worth $16.2 billion in 2010," PCR, 3/2/2011. http://www.pcr-online.biz. Retrieved 1/25/2012.

Chapter 15: Have The Mayans Ever Lied To You?

Tedlock, Barbara. "Time and the Highland Maya" Revised edition (1992) p. 1.

Miles, Susanna W, "An Analysis of the Modern Middle American Calendars: A Study in Conservation." In Acculturation in the Americas. Edited by Sol Tax, pp. 283-84. Chicago: University of Chicago Press, 1952.

Coe, Michael D. *Breaking the Maya Code*. (London: Thames & Hudson 1992).

Bonander, Ross. "2012: 5 Things You Didn't Know." AskMen.com. http://www.askmen.com/entertainment/special_feature_300/374b_2012-5-things-you-didnt-know. Retrieved 8/27/2010. Speigel, Lee. "Doomsday: After Many Predictions, We're Still Here." http://www.aolnews.com/2011/01/06/doomsday-after-many-predictions-were-still-here/. Retrieved 1/11/2011.

"Massive solar storm to hit Earth in 2012 with 'force of 100m bombs.'" Yahoo!News. http://in.news.yahoo.com/139/20100826/981/tsc-massive-solar-storm-to-hit-earth-in_1.html. Retrieved 8/27/2010.

Cookson, Clive. "Scientists warn of $2,000bn solar 'Katrina.' FT.com. http://www.ft.com.cms/s/0/67444b2c-3d13-11e0-bbff-00144feabdc0.html. Retrieved 2/21/2011.

Also By Robert Stricklin

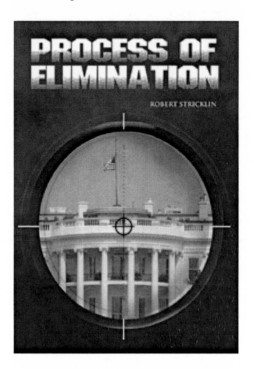

Process of Elimination

On a bright Saturday morning in May, the nation is jolted by the news that the Vice President of the United States has perished in a plane crash. After a respectable period of mourning, President James J. Hartman begins the arduous task of vetting and choosing a successor. But as White House correspondent Gideon Burnett soon learns, forces intent on undermining the administration are plotting to influence the President's decision - by any means necessary. What is their ultimate agenda? And can Burnett expose the plot in time before he becomes a target for elimination?

Learn more at: www.outskirtspress.com/Processofelimination

CPSIA information can be obtained at www.ICGtesting.com
Printed in the USA
LVOW122054040412

276206LV00003B/134/P